ARC OF THE ANCIENTS

AND
OTHER POETRY
© 1994-2003

Including the Circle of Life Poetry Collection
©1978-1987

THE ALMOST COMPLETE POETRY
COLLECTIONS
OF
M A R T I N . A . E N T I C K N A P

ARC OF THE ANCIENTS
AND OTHER POETRY
copyright © 1994-2003 by Martin A. Enticknap

Including the Circle of Life Poetry Collection
copyright ©1978-1987 by Martin A. Enticknap

First published printing: April 2003

color cover wraparound illustration created by
Martin A. Enticknap
copyright © 2002 by Martin A. Enticknap

book cover layout by: Brian Matthews
Jobsoft Design and Development Inc.
Murfreesboro, Tennessee

ISBN: 1-928798-34-9

type: Poetry

ARC OF THE ANCIENTS is a print-on-demand title with Ingram Book Company.
Copies are available through:
bookstore orders and also through
http://www.Amazon.co.uk and
http://www.amazon.com

Armstrong Valley Publishing Company
Murfreesboro, Tennessee USA

printed in Great Britain or in the United States of America

Dedicated to
My Brother James
For his understanding of the five-fold pattern...

And to my other brothers and Sisters

Susan, Laura, Sharon, David and Gary.

**And to my Granddad Herbert Enticknap
and to Granddad Jack Jones**
Who may have passed on thirty-five and twenty years ago
but still have an impact on my life.

And finally to the Isle and people of Sanday.

Acknowledgements must be made to
Robert S. Sanders, Jr., whose friendship has been an inspiration
and without whom this collection would not have been
published. To my online friends from the Dome, and other
writers sites who have read and enjoyed most of the poems and
work in this collection, in particular to Suzzie, Cat, Dipps,
Ossian, Whynot, Julie, Asterix, Mez, Jane, Jenny, Brian,
Mist&Fog, Kazzie, Angie, Di, Ian, Cheryl, Victoria and many
more too numerous to mention but you know who you are!
Also a mention to a few others friends who have inspired some
of this work like dearest Maureen, Carole and Jack, Simone and
Jack, Dave and the Scribblers for your friendship means more
than you can know. Also to Eileen, Dawn and her family, never
forgotten and always a place in my heart.

And Finally to Jen and Cassie,
The reason for light that continues to inspire and delight me,
My life would not be the same, with all my love.

**NOTE: There is a second dedication page for the second half of this complete
works.**

Arc of the Ancients Cover

ARC OF THE ANCIENTS
And Other Poetry
CONTENTS

Athena
Magic Isle
No Shadow Falls
Purple Passion
Eternal Kiss
The Cup
Wolfen Heart
Winter Snow
To Play The Dream
Giant's Lament

Falling Angel
The Dance Of Souls
In The Rain
Missing You In Time
I Had A Dream...
Doorway
Faith
Sand Kiss
Unicorn Dance
Shield Of Love

Between Heart Beats
Alien Commingled
Cold Lullaby
Holocaust
Making Planets
Pockets Full Of Sand
Just Mad
The Lamenting Corpse
Riding The Pale Horse
Ruminations Of Vomit
I.D.I.O.T.
Walking In My Blood
Kyrie Eleison
Dark Clock
"It's Almost Time To Go Home"
Funeral Of Lilly & Then Cho
Dolphin Kind
A Ripple In Focus
Pennine Contact
Sleeping Among The Stars
Beyond Heaven

Staring Into The Eyes OF Eternity

THREE PERSPECTIVES ON THE WORK AND THE MAN
1.

I am deeply honoured to be invited to write an Introduction to this soul stirring Poetry Collection. On the day I met Martin a flame was lit, a flame that burns ever brightly in my heart and in my soul and cannot be extinguished. That catalytic meeting set me on a spiritual journey during which we have shared a myriad of precious and treasured memories, which I can dip into at, will. I feel that this book contains a myriad of poems and other writings, which you can dip into whenever you want to touch your soul with their evocative magic – with something special and very different. Listen to their harmonies and their wisdom with your spirit and share some moments in time with the poet. Sometimes you'll find your perceptions challenged, sometimes you'll feel inspired, sometimes you'll be enchanted, sometimes you'll be uplifted, sometimes you'll feel the wisdom, sometimes you'll share a precious moment, sometimes you'll feel spiritual, sometimes you'll be moved to tears and sometimes you'll laugh but you'll not remain untouched.

My first impression of Martin was of a very 'old soul' full of wisdom – the eyes are the mirror of the soul and the warmth and wisdom of his spirit certainly shone through his eyes as it does through his poems. He was then only 24 years old. I was soon to discover that he was a very talented and accomplished Poet whose poetry I would come to love and enjoy even more than that that of my old favourites Blake, Shelley and Byron. Martin's thought provoking and inspirational poems are from the soul and they rarely fail to touch the spirit deeply.

The painful memories of his childhood would have drowned the spirit of many a person but his indomitable spirit was not quenched and he came through it all as a shining example of the strength of the spirit to rise above it all, to move forward and learn from the circle of life. Some of this personal journey is captured in *The Circle of Life Poetry Collection*, which was written before we met and is here published in its original form to illustrate the natural evolution of his poetry.

I consider the *Arc of the Ancients* collection of poems that includes the *Prologue to Arc of the Ancients Series, Arc of the Ancients – Invocation of the Paradigm a Series* and *Epilogue to Arc of the Ancients* to be a truly brilliant, thought provoking and prophetic body of work. When I first read them I thought of them as 21st century prophecies but then realized that would not do them justice because they showed humanity's present situation as well as foreseeing the possibilities for the future. *The 911 Aftermath Poems* follow this and are very poignant whilst again showing the possibilities.

The poems show a true understanding of life and humanity in all its diversity and complexities. They show what has been, what is and what could be. The work of a Visionary. The wider issues confronting humanity on its spiritual journey are confronted in the *Arc of the Ancients* but really I can't put it better than to use the poet's own words from the final two verses of Quantum *Redux* i.e.

The heritage of the Arc of the Ancients is a warning,
A gift and a reminder that each step you take,
Touches the world once gross and subtle,
Each an invocation of the paradigm,
In the eternal journey of the soul.

A revolution is occurring,
You may not see it but you will feel it,
When the fivefold pattern is born in your heart,
Lighting your mind to the possibilities of your soul,
A reflection on eternity - the face of the Quantum Redux...

This should give you a taste of what is to come but I would also like to quote some lines from another poem *Miracle in the Darkness* because it says much about the ethos of this collection.

Time to choose a different way and make a true
Miracle from the light that is the hope,
That lies waiting to be upheld.

To unite in humanity, to unite in diversity,
To unite our hopes and fears in peace.

The next section *The Saga Poems* are written in the Bardic tradition. Martin is adept at painting pictures with his words and you can let yourself flow within the horizons of these poems.

The Far to the Right of Magic Poems weave a richly magical and mystical tapestry of shimmering colours. These poems will take you into other realms where your perceptions will be challenged.

A Rainbow of Love Poems is a beautiful collection of poems and you will find much to touch your soul here. Relax and enjoy.

The Otherside of Midnight Poems is such an extremely diverse and fascinating kaleidoscope of poems that it would be impossible to categorize them so I suggest you explore them for yourself. It will be worth it!

The poignancy of the *Final Reflection Poems* will touch your heart in ways that will move you to tears.

And finally when you want a rest from poems there are *The BloodFire* stories and the short story entitled A *Christmas Time Story* and there is more besides.

JEN
Wednesday, 05 March 2003

<u>2.</u>

A Journey of Life

Take a peek into life, into the heart and soul of a being that transcends realities. Experience the colours of warmth and love, the colours of the cold, the myriad shades of emotions, soulful warmth of happiness and joy, the sadness of sorrow and pain. A paradox of collisions of many peoples that have impacted this human's life, the expression of compassion and forgiveness of the misdemeanours of others, and the gratitude for their gifts. Taste the absorption of myriad experiences, fused and moulded into a unique individual, see the questions and challenges that have been posed and expressed in this collective gallery of thoughts, feelings and expressions.

Understand and see the pure constant of his desire and zest for Truth & Hope. Feel the merging of realities, the spontaneous revelations, the virgin birth of ideas, the breath of fresh air that blows across your mind and soul, originating from the fearless pursuit of his own sense of purpose, his confronting of self doubts and belief in Hope. Watch the ebb and flow his own current, guiding him through the storms of the past, guiding him to the calm of his own wisdom.

See the conjunction of experiences and the learning of a Great Song, the music that plays through us all that transcends the physical, the heart and soul of this special individual that has chosen to share in his myriad perspectives on himself and us all. See the leap of faith from loathing to sheer love of all things in this life and the many things of life that we don't see with our eyes, but can feel with our heart. Be like a drop of water which falls from the sky above which drops into the collective ocean of life, taking the twist and turns as the currents and eddies taking this drop on a journey through all the oceans, up the rivers and their tributaries, feel what's it like to fall over the edge of eternal waterfall, to cascade from a great height to the waiting warmth of the lake below, journey with this soul my friends and partake in this feast of life! Alpha Omega Alpha!

JAMES
Thursday, 06 March 2003
Dedicated to M.A.D. for his pure dedication to life!

3.

Martin is a star in the real and profound meaning of the word; he sheds a bright light for others to see by. He isn't a teacher but his life has become 'a teaching'. On the Internet and The Dome, Martin's poetry is eagerly awaited even though there may be tears as well as smiles when we read it.

Many people, including myself have been inspired by how he lives his life. Despite physical pain and sickness, he produces poetry layered with meaning and filled with beauty, compassion and humour. His poems are a look into a rare and precious soul and I and everyone who comes into contact with him are privileged and enriched by that meeting.

As Walt Whitman said, 'Camerado,' this is no book you hold. *'This is a man'*

SUZZIE, Queen of The Pleasure Dome a Home for Writers on MSN

Thursday, 06 March 2003

Arc of The Ancients

A PROLOGUE TO THE SERIES

-1-
PARADIGM

Chaos pattern evolving true form,
In the depths where atoms decide,
To challenge the status quo of the tired.
Flowing new strength into inspirational,
Hologrammatical matter in human expression.

The cosmic fire that is an undulation,
Of rippling colourful oscillating blooms.
Juxtaposing soul to molecules of life,
Vibrating to make the invitation,
Of the changing season upon them all.

Lifting eyes from the dark loam,
To gaze in awe at what they are.
To see how truly magical a soul,
Can be when attention is given,
Freely to life's glorious pattern.

Tasting heaven when all is dark,
Within the silence the music
Of kindness to those that can't find.
The heart to love those that hate,
A world that is reshaping us all.

-2-
FINAL DAYS

Withdrawing behind concrete walls,
The legions of the lost depart to stand.
While the flesh of the innocent are burnt away,
The land is closed to all who would dare to wonder.

Shut behind the noise of infinite TV screens,
Listening to the lies that are wrapped as truth for that day.
While the blood sacrifice is made to bring power,
To the one who would be the final Caesar in their desiccated play.

The sky fills with wonders that no eyes will ever see,
While the third age of Rome struggles not to fade.
When the might is paid by dirty coin to plunder,
The mouths that gape like silent thunder.

To speak a word that makes their walls tremble,
Will find you bound by chains for the new arena.
Sacrificed for the desires that wish to see blood in your eyes,
Even as you see them stain their snow of winter.

New legions are being fortified so glory,
Can be claimed against those they armed.
Like push button toy soldiers to me melted,
In the fires of their children's future.

Like fools in many coloured cloaks,
There are ten heads of the Hydra that wish to be.
The one to bring a new standard held aloft to proclaim,
They're right to be Caesar in the coming final days.

Arc of The Ancients
Invocation of the Paradigm
A series...

-1-

FOOTSTEPS OF GAIA

There can be no more time for tears,
No more mopping the brow and wringing hands for the dead.
In her footsteps you can see the potential,
The power that is yours to wield in the making of a new thread.

Allow the call that is seeping up from the earth,
To bathe your hands in the soil and feel the wisdom that she demands.
That you become the footsteps that she has shown you,
To stand tall against those coming to turn the fields blood red.

The silence is only the beginning in the debt you owe,
No more idle hands but the threads that you are ordained to be.
In the weave that is your strength to be the banner,
That will fly in the face of the walking dead.

Your life is bound to every footstep she takes,
When she bleeds you shall bleed.
Her wounds are your wounds,
When she dies you die too.

So it is written, so it shall be done.

So the steps begin...[1]

---

[1] This poem was First published in India 2002 By CyberWit In The Anthology of World Poetry – *The Golden Wings*

-2-
THE LEGACY OF YSBADDADEN

From the Castle that is lost in the shroud of history,
To Legend and Myth drowning the grief of a King.
Who time has repainted as a beast under the flag,
Of the cross and the vanity of a hero whom knelt
Before his cousin Arthur the Once and future King.

Shining mirrors distort the image so lust can take,
The daughter from her father the King of all the Giants.
From the mountains to the forest and seas,
Of a Briton basking under the shimmer of summer sun
Beginning the lies that bite the carcass of this once and future land.

The roar of a wronged soul who begins the long climb back,
To stand once more on the grey granite peak to survey.
The legacy and to repay the debt a land now owes,
In the compliance of a man who claims the crown
That proclaims the right of a man who stole a father's heart.

If mortal Man's grief can last a lifetime,
Then the grief of a Giant can last for eternity.
Bringing a legacy that reaches to clasp the shoulder of history,
For the demand to be heard and reclaim what was lost.
So that the tears can be shed to cleanse the land,
Of the poison that hides the true face of history.

Will his tears be rocks that fall from the sky?
Or rivers that overflow their banks.
To the snow of winter breaking the back of spring,
Or the shudder and creak of a land so soaked in blood
That it may open wide to release those painful cries.

If a legend were reborn would you rush to hold the banner?
Watch it unfurl as your children wait in arms.
To steal the heart of another in the name of heroes,
Called from the depth of a repainted history.
To fight in a War that will end all wars,
One more time is all they will ask.

4

Be warned the colours of history paint the canvas,
Of this future until we listen to those who lost.
Everything to the lies of a legend wrapped in the blood,
Of those that kneel at the feet of
A recoated Once and Future King.

So the steps continue....

So it is written, so it shall be done...

-3-
THE MAKING OF ANGAKUK

The time of conclusion had stirred the wonders,
To search in the snow-white landscape for the embodiment
Of the first heart to be the drum to sound the warning.
That there was nowhere to run,
No new sea to fish.
No new wind to fly away upon,
No new crisp virgin land to flourish upon.

Impact on a startled heart caught the cry as a choking sob,
From a child scraping the arid dust for the first grain
In the shadow of a flag of cooling stars.
Even as a fool tugs on a dragon's tail,
And plays the oldest end game with a Trojan plane.

Then the first walk away from all that was known,
With the vapour of magic a contrail to begin
The reshaping to expose the cracks in the armour of the mighty.
To understand that there is only one land, sea and sky,
That none should forsake the wisdom when the last bell tolls.

The gates are swung open to empty the last children,
Upon the streets as they know that school has ended.
No more time for playground games,
No more time for playground bullies,
No more time for the playground taunts.
Time to end the misery of those that are different,
That make everyone alone and weak.

Even as the clarity of vision makes the glass the prism,
That breaks light it allows the reason to be.
Swimming in the ever-increasing circle of deceit,
When children carry guns and proud parents scream.
Their hatreds to poison the waters to become the,
Cries that they will weep as their children are cut down in the streets.

Those that were, that are and those that will be,
Grew as magic in the heart they had chosen.
But a question formed upon widening lips,
Even as the vision of what was, what are and what might well be.
Became the warning star embedded in the golden face,
Of all the gods that were, that are, that will never to be.

"Where is the vision of those that could be?"

It was a question that they couldn't answer,
It was beyond the scope of those that whispered.
In the wind, in the roar of the ocean and the movement of the earth,
But they had inspired the question in the making.
Now they could leave and allow the answer,
To grow from those that could be.

Those yet to be classified,
Those growing silently in the wings
They will create the landscape that has never been.

This is the voice that haunts the dreams of those that scream,
That only they have dominion over those they see
In the fields, in the sky, in the oceans and streets.

So the steps continue...

So it is written, so it shall be done.

-4-
ECHO OF THE TITANS

Deep in slumber the shadow stretches,
Far beneath the concrete jungles of Man.
To the captured open spaces where freedom,
Is bestowed by hallowed voices lost in their heaven.

Stirs the fire of forgotten voices to break the silence,
Of those waiting to loosen the grip of Gaia's first children.
To gain the riches by darkening the sky with black gold,
As they believe in the right bestowed by their unforgiving law.

So it swells with liquid fire to break free as she stirs,
The memory of Olympus first betrayal to be the seed.
To let all know that an echo can still teach,
That time is the illusion of perspective willing to be.

Upon a wave it travels to bear a message to the depth,
Where blood runs swift to stir Oceanus in his great sleep.
To dream a dream that will haunt those which wait,
For the order to collide on a red and blue ochre sea.

Breaking the surface to shape a face to scowl,
Upon the islands that are hiding a generation.
In the fascination of a world built from castles of sand,
That will shift under them when the winds turn northeast.

Across the tapestry to an embroiled land,
Fighting of a family that has its roots from the same tree.
Where prophecy has become the lie to reshape the heart,
Born to lay the foundation of those who claim to be free.

Breaking with axes the stones splattered with blood,
Tearing up the heart that was founded upon a wish.
To rip at the throat of the image swirling in the holy font,
The final reflection of those who built their God from sand.

Creating the vibration that becomes the wave of particles,
To loosen the fingers of Atlas in the struggle to be free.
Breaking the chains of eons to walk away from the burden,
Set by children who craved the power of never ending dominion.

So fades the echo of the Titans,
As they bow from mythology to history in a timeless dream.
Leaving the footprints as a reminder in the souls of those,
Who would dare to create a future from the shadows
That should be left as reflections of history.

So the steps continue....

So it is written, so it shall be done...

-5-
APEX OF THE ARC

The sun shines brighter to melt the snow of winter,
Upon the heights of this mountain that is the island
Surrounded by the cooling waters of the open sea.
Turning to see the truth mirrored in the reflection of,
Times eternal twin standing facing the millennium sun.

It was whispered in the drying blood that invoked,
The fracture that would be thorns in the words
Of the book that cleansed the truth from the,
Vision found on the mountain that is twinned
To the isle of flowers under the purple reign of stars.

Sitting in dust under a barren sun thirsting for the green,
In the secrets that is seen in the flowers flowing down
To the sea that calls the heart of the twin sitting on the shore.
For the answer to a question that fooled eighty generations,
That looked for the truth in the agony that haunts them all.

The codex that held a simple truth was never written,
Only a hand across the timeless ribbon would reach
To grasp the focus in the grip of flesh never touched but felt.
Making a mountain in the desert reach the shore of a summer,
In the truth scrawled upon the foam breached silver sand.

8

ARC OF THE ANCIENTS

The sand became the hourglass trickling away time,
As footsteps returned to a land held by the grip
Of the purple cloth devoid of future silver stars.
So they could choose what they will with an innocent heart,
On the rock never kissed by cool breathe of an open sea.

When the call of why that broke the hearts of those,
That witnessed the end of colours painted from a dream
Echoed through the walkways of time to the hesitant beat.
Of the one who had held out the hand to give courage,
In the darkness under so much light - time could only collide.

One heart broken by the faithless under the desert sun,
Another breaking by the hopelessness of a lost dream
Slowly beating under the shattering pain to the crimson haze.
Creating reflections to touch the world in the grains of sand,
Passing from the one who died to the one who returned...

So the steps continue....

So it is written, so it shall be done...

-6-
MARE TENEBROSUM

No moon or stars can shine in the eternity of darkness,
That waits to claim those who sail upon a becalmed sea.
The screams will never be heard of those that wail,
Huddled below deck sickened by cancerous despair.

Faces but a memory, just the heat and stench of breath,
Gagging on the cries sinking hope to run as rats in the night.
Chewing on numb fingers and blackened toes,
Waiting for the fresh wind to cleanse more than soul.

Chains rattle as the boards creak with the thud,
Of leather-clad footsteps of those who know the fate.
Of those who cry to live before landfall in the promised land,
In the slavery of freedom bonded by the strength of flesh.

In the one who returned is a lost smile in the darkness,
That does not scream as fleas bite among the curses.
Knowing flesh is but the motion of the mind lost in focus,
Using the silence of soul turning blindness into sight.

Frustration turns as glittering metal unsheathed,
To bite the hearts of mutiny as red as the cloaks.
Of those that believe in the mastery of their race,
Oblivious to the silence that now reigns below their feet.

A small fire burns as mind spread the wings of soul,
To spark the nearest breaking the chains of flesh.
Empathy the kiss of compassion lighting five hundred,
Hearts to the power of life floating on a sea of darkness.

The concert of mind singing in harmony creating,
An azure light softly glowing and faces lost are now found.
Among the dirt, the blood and rags are a people,
Who are no longer bowed but standing as iron chains fall.

The guardians of an empire encrusted with salt and grime,
Upon a sea paused, waiting for a history to be defined.
With unbelieving eyes they turn towards the azure light rising,
Blood running cold as a lost people find their voice and Cry,

"We are the Paradigm..
                              And this is how it begins..."

So the steps continue....

So it is written, so it shall be done...

-7-
QUANTUM REDUX

From the Pyramids to the magical stone circles of the north,
To the ancient ruins and temples of those that wrote,
In pictures and signs of a dream that broke through.
Claiming the hearts and souls of those touched by the catalyst,
That sung the song bidding them to mark the notes,
Of a metacreative wave upon the ocean for those to come.

The concert of the metaphysical is a hungry song,
More complex than the colours of light freeing souls.
To leap across the divide of material space to shake the hands,
Clasped in the willingness of faith more than reason,
Linking those unseen in a bond stronger than bricks and mortar.

In inner space the five fold pattern is spontaneously born,
So round are the squares that sparkle with humour,
Eternal in grace riding the stream through a crystal city.
Each facet a colour from light to darkness is a sublime face,
Touching the outstretched fingers of those who wish to know.

Reformation of the tranquillity of storms in the hidden heart,
The mellow silence that is open to the diversity of the soul,
In the dreams that drive the intent to listen to the world unseen.
More than blood and flesh is this desire to communicate,
An idea more delicate then the pattern in the heart of a flower.

This journey can never end each step is a link in a movement,
Like a daisy chain worn by a child under a summer sun.
Innocent of the fire that is waiting to burn away care free days,
When illusions are blown away by the storms eroding the sand,
From a face that will haunt those choosing to witness and stay.

The heritage of the Arc of the Ancients is a warning,
A gift and a reminder that each step you take,
Touches the world once gross and subtle,
Each an invocation of the paradigm,
In the eternal journey of the soul.

A revolution is occurring,
You may not see it but you will feel it,
When the fivefold pattern is born in your heart,
Lighting your mind to the possibilities of your soul,
A reflection on eternity - the face of the Quantum Redux...

So the steps continue....

So it is written, so it shall be done...

EPILOGUE TO ARC OF THE ANCIENTS SERIES

-1-

Alpha - Omega - Alpha

One path known in the beginning full of twists and turns,
The sculpture seen in all its glory by touch.
Desires to be the face seen in the mystery of a glistening
Perfectly flawed soap bubble.

The cry of the baby enraged to be born,
With the sight to see the world as it truly is.
A gift unbidden to gaze upon those that speak,
In grey tones of decaying dust.

Seasons march on as the world fills with empty spaces,
Screaming softly we come in peace.
Making ears itch and hearts to drop,
As bombs covered in roses smelling so sweet.

Gather judges like precious flowers to pass the sentence,
While those protected by divinity of the winning side smile.
Sailing upon the sea of unwanted and forgotten crimes,
Sowing a thousand million more tombstone cries.

By the power invested in the righteous slyest grin,
Democratically parting the limbs from those that didn't know.
A thousand million eyes waiting to see the drool,
Betraying the unguarded moment to be sacrificed on TV.

ARC OF THE ANCIENTS

The blood sacrifice is the making of order from chaos,
To fall upon those that would dare to breach the temple.
To walk among them to turn the face of the world away,
To brand those that would dare spoil this brave new world.

Gather a thousand experts and watch as they spin,
Cobwebs of truth that are shattered by a mountain roar.
Are Illusions of abstract order dictated by the unimaginative,
Broken by the red-hot passion of rock to be free.

The sun rises to cook languid smiling happy flesh.
Nothing can be wrong for the reflection would know,
That the scythe has the right time and the earth wouldn't dare,
To fall beneath such carefully observed feet.

As fast as it is consumed the blood needs replenishing,
Or the signal they dread will come to pass.
When the shuffling decay fails to smile once more,
On those lost to the pyramid of divine power.

Now walk the empty spaces of rooms leading to souls,
Guarding their zealous secrets in the failures of ritual.
Then with heart felt compassion pull the random string,
And watch...

Alpha - Omega - Alpha

Fire will light the moon...

So the steps pause to wait,
To see....

So it is written...
So it now begins...[2]

---

[2] *[THIS IS THE FINAL POEM IN THE ARC OF THE ANCIENTS SERIES, WHICH WERE WRITTEN FROM JUNE 2000 TO JUNE 2001 AND WERE A WARNING OF WHAT WAS TO COME... ALL TEN POEMS WERE POSTED ON THE INTERNET[2] IN VARIOUS PLACES WHEN WRITTEN. THIS IS THE FIRST TIME THEY HAVE APPEARED TOGETHER IN ONE PUBLICATION.]*

THE 911 AFTERMATH POEMS

-1-
MIRACLE IN THE DARKNESS

We know that the sky fell,
That sunshine was swallowed by the clouds,
That kissed the ground.
We know that tens of thousands didn't die on that day,
Yet we wait to bury the thousands who did.
The story of survival is the hope in the time that waits,
For those that hunger to see the face,
To come home and share their miracle in the darkness.

We know that no matter how many times,
We run in this tortuous circle,
Not all can be brought safely home.
But there is magic to be found in that day,
In all the dusty tear streaked faces that returned.

We walk among them in our dreams,
Those that can never turn the page,
But their lives are our miracle waiting to be,
That the tears of loss don't become the reason,
We choose to make the sky fall on those,
Who will have to live in hope to survive once again?

Rather than building a stone cenotaph for a war,
That is declared let us build a peace.
Where we can say its time to unlock the shackles,
Of fear to open our hearts to the possibilities.
To understand why we make landscapes,
That others would choose to fall in fear upon.

No matter how it is told it was and never will be,
About one man who mirrors the fear in the eyes,
Of those that wish to have dominion.
But about the fear that hides in the darker places,
In all our hearts.

14

ARC OF THE ANCIENTS

For those that died and those that survived,
In their name can it not be the day we chose differently.
And not stain their memory by declaring that,
This day was the first day in a 21st century war.
But rather the day we all took responsibility,
For what was, what is, and what is to come.
Time to choose a different way and make a true
Miracle from the light that is the hope,
That lies waiting to be upheld.

To unite in humanity, to unite in diversity,
To unite our hopes and fears in peace.[3]

-2-

THE CRUCIBLE OF CHANGES

From East to West, from North to South,
The winds roared in with passions aflame.
To mark the place that had been chosen to bear,
The child whose eyes will witness the crucible of changes.

The soul as ancient as the will to know examines the choices,
From those who cloak the face of truth in the lies of heritage.
In all the layers of secular and religious agendas,
The hunger to be recognised as the one is the passion that grows.

The winds of winter blow across a land of hollows,
The night sky lit by the flashes that mark the fear of a world
That will decide the fate of a child who can only wonder,
In whose name it will have to die for.

But in the reflection of fire many faces stare back,
Those who have to decide if the fate of the many
Will be dictated by the few who have already decided,
In the hollow shell of democratic freedom and holy dogma.

---

[3] In Memory of Tuesday 11th of September 2001

In the sand a hungry dry finger traces all roads,
In the centre they meet and in horror they share the same face.
A child sees them as twins sharing one body tearing itself apart,
In anger and frustration for how could they be one and the same?

In simple faith the child wishes not to die tonight,
In hope it wishes that the twins would set aside their blood stained cloaks.
Rest their stolen crowns upon the sand and admit the truth,
That they do not speak for the world or the God they proclaim.

The child is almost forgotten now - resting its cheek upon the sand,
Watching the fires burn brighter and brighter and wonders...
Just as another child in whose name wondered if it would be safe,
Even as the towers fell and the future became a wind swept dust cloud.

Unknown...open... isn't it?

-3-

FAITH DEEP IN THE RESTING ARMS...

Faith deep in the resting arms of possibility is never silent,
While shadows try to shape the world in your perfect image.
But like many before the flaws hidden in the glass are felt,
By the curious hands that wonder just who made you the voice of God.

Sculpting a future from the fears of those that witness the end,
The assassination of dreams that show the temporary nature of a child.
Keeping the hand tight on the idea of divine right when the spirit cries,
That the words are lies founded on a political agenda.

But a war created to combat terror is hollow if you make all bend their knee,
To the idea that the enemy is a dark god and not just a sick pitiful man.
Who was once your partner and a friend who negotiated with the state,
To unlock the possibilities of an oil pipeline from a landlocked sea.

ARC OF THE ANCIENTS

When the architect of terror is created by those that had the power to see,
It falls that you cannot be blameless if your hands are soaked in blood.
Reshaping a world like clay all you can make is stained and destined to fall,
Even as you gather the way to cull people like sheep that you see them to
be.

Easy to shine the light that blinds those that upholds you in power,
To pass the holy writ that takes away freedom from all that refuse your
piety.
Proclaiming justice will be served that fears will be no more,
When you can inoculate against the idea that they have a right to choose.

You can wrap in a million distractions of fear to keep them chattering,
In hope that that the crucible you created will serve to bind them in chains.
That the ripples of footsteps are just an illusion and no one will bring you,
The news that the people have torn your paper tiger to pieces.

The terrible truth is that your world no longer exists,
It ended when the times were changed to give you pause.
A millennium dance to allow you to choose and you chose unwisely,
To continue to play the game of great powers to build an elite world order.

Based on the handclasps of tyrants and butchers recast in your image,
Praying that you will win your 21st century war upheld by their gory
glorious hands.
Free to broaden a war in arrogant assurance that the people will never
notice,
The diseases that you unleashed in the name of freedom and justice.

But you didn't pay attention to the possibility,
That your worldview can no longer be sustained.
Because you choose not to consider the price that will be paid,
When you believe you can sell our humanity so cheaply.

Faith deep in the arms of possibility has already spoken...

THE SAGA POEMS

-1-

MALKARI'S REQUIEM

I was born into darkness,
Everyday a darkscape.
A lonely vista,
A rivened land.
But for within the night a rainbow of colour lit the heavens,
A dance that lifted and drew colour into my soul
A burning flame for all to behold.
For all who knowest me,
In this land of tortured soul.

Everyday was my night,
Every night my salvation
The strangest nightlight of all.
I can imagine what you have seen,
For I stood there facing you
Did you not see ?
I know of all that you are,
Your fire burns into me
A raging sea.
That turns me inside out,
A holocaust being born.
This is a truth we share,
The silver voice of all shown unto me.
The wisdom of your fire,
The birth of a child running wild into the flame
A living beacon of light.

I felt it burning,
My eyes cauterised.
My ears shrivelled,
My lips blackened.
My tongue just a crisp,
My face burnt away.

ARC OF THE ANCIENTS

My terrified cries,
Enough to break any heart that cared to listen.

When my cries of terror were silenced,
My body torn asunder by exploding flame.
Between the darkness and the rainbow,
That blew me as kisses of fire.
So I could see the lies and truth,
Terror and salvation.
For when I was no more,
Now silent and still.
That I felt myself within the holocaust of fire,
That rained down upon me.
Did I finally learn to listen and learn,
What should remain unthought and untold.
What should be told and thought,
In the paradox of fire.

In the shadow of soul,
I heard and saw the dark futures.
Over an ever increasing expanse,
From the dawn of ages
To all the ages old.
The power grows to hold the minds of mortal things,
Their screams as they become light of their darkness
The paradox of confusion.
The frightened souls blinded by the truth,
Of what they refuse to behold.

Across the battlefield my shadow falls,
No words - No sight
No ears to divert me.
Until I felt you all as shadow,
Your silence is a truth
Waiting to burn from your souls.
Thus I am before you,
As a bloody dawn arises
The rainbow of the birthing fire.
To confuse and consume the unwary,
With you I see the unthinkable revealed
With only you my soul grows new eyes.

As is the truth I found,
When the screams of my terror were stripped away.

Did I find the courage to be still,
Thus I behold the Game as it begins.
The first pieces,
The lives and land
The cities - The lights
The pieces of hope.
Flow - wander - scream,
To vanish as the fires found them.
The ebb and flow of Ages,
That rise and fall
Of mortal works.
Of the struggle to silence their screams upon the field,
Of dark and light that their pieces march.

From within to without the Game is played,
The souls journey from earth as is to heaven
This is their given.
The separation to break the Arch of time,
To shatter the soul of all unto the play.
Upon the misbegotten field,
To lay huddled within your dead dark and cold cities.
The cup emptied,
The grail thrown upon the ground
As they find their heaven into hell.
But if they could see the lie within the truth,
The truth within the lie they would scream,
Once more for their folly.

I remember standing before you all,
As I stand now and as I will always stand.
Until the pattern of dreams and nightmares,
Reach unto the enchantment of all imagined heavens as could be.
When they know that,
This is only the beginning of wisdom.

My song endeth here,
If you see within me a pure light.
Look to see the weave of darkness,
See the silver web that is us both.
Thus the reflection within my tears,
Can show you your true face.
That your darkness is a flame of silver too,
Thus this is when a soul giveth birth to paradox.....

ARC OF THE ANCIENTS

The opposite and the same,
The light and darkness just reflections.
Of soul as they meet the challenge,
To weave heavens fire with the darkness of below.
The silver truth of Gold,
To initiate the hope that dwells within us all. [4]

-2-

STONECARVER

On every eleventh morn the rich aroma awakens her,
Across the castle grounds she runs - her white night shift,
A flashing beacon for all those that saw her.
Knowing she was rushing to witness the magic,
That brought life from cold stone.

Under the overhang of red-pottered tile roof he sat,
No other tool just his hands resting lightly upon a square block.
Until it began to ripple causing hot spicy steam,
That quickly arose around him.
Changing everything into a secret shadow world,
With her safe inside with chin on her knees entranced
Waiting - still as un-worked stone.

Watching stone melt under his hands like the purest honey,
He could feel her eyes watching the caress of stone.
Feeling the image escape the confines of the vacuity,
Her silver blue eyes smiled under a shock of golden hair.
As a leg smooth of calf shook free as his hands slewed,
Aside the warm slick marble paste no longer hardened stone.

No words could ever be spoken,
In the long years only silence could be,
While she grew into a maiden ready to be Queen.

---

[4] *This poem has been soundscaped and is available direct from the Author as a MP3 file- a very spooky choir and wolves soundtrack!*

So he watched her knowing that soon she would be taken,
To a foreign land fall of empty strangers.
But he knew that a word would spell his doom,
For he was slave to the whims of her father.
Not for him to know her warm silken touch,
Just the work that brought another life from stone.

His hands knotted brown to tapered figure tips,
Caressed an ankle delicate china white to five wriggling toes.
She giggled as she wondered if she would ever know that touch,
With a deep crimson blush - hiding for a moment.
Then to gasp as gossamer wings suddenly fluttered,
Between delicate pale white shoulders,
As the figure struggled to be free of stone.

Deeper his fingers dug while his eyes watched her,
Feeling the heat rise inside as fingers plucked.
A head with a shock of white hair that shook,
Free to turn and gaze upon the likeness that cried in glee.
Every line perfect in the nakedness his heart had seen,
His last gift to the gentle princess that sat entranced.
As the fairy stretched on tiptoe and fluttered her wings,
To smile - a wink - a dance upon his knee,
This had been his decree - life from stone.

Everything shattered,
The intimacy of their world broken.
The silence defeated by the clash of steel,
Her shock as her father broke into a run towards her.
Dust all grey billowed as horses reared,
The fear as she turned back to see the look,
Of horror as the Castle shook - fire beginning to fall.
The spell truly broken - the magic fleeing,
The fairy falling to be shattered as life leaves stone.

His eyes glistened as the tiny smile that was her likeness,
Was scattered into dust as he rose to protect her.
There was no time as the King pulled her a way,
And the Knights called all to arms.
Over tan leather silver amour was quickly strapped,
Now no longer a carver of stone,
But a man at arms - to fight for a feeble king,
Whose heart would never know the strength of stone.

ARC OF THE ANCIENTS

She had tried to look but soon she was lost,
In a melee of fear and cries that tore the heart,
From a orange darkened sky.
Her white shift torn from her - as maids quickly dressed,
In a blood red - the outfit that would rob her dreams.
To be anything other than a Queen that would never know,
The touch of the man who brought life to stone.

He fought with sword and shield,
Blood staining the cobbled street.
Screams like notes torn from the tower bell,
Filled his head but his heart only yearned,
To see once more his quiet soulful princess.
So the magic could once more sing,
To the lives hidden in the depth of stone.

Wood splintered by iron axes,
The door ravaged as chain mail covered hands,
Tore apart so they could take the prize.
Waiting in the soft cloth of mellow red,
Who stood while those gathered now ran.
In shrouds of fear they abandoned a princess,
Who knew that nothing would save her.
While the man who had touched her soul,
Fought with steel instead of the freeing the heart in stone.

With sails like cotton free upon the wind,
Ships filled the harbour beyond the gate.
Spilling men with beasts as foam flowing,
From a tankard of poisoned mead.
Ten score by ten they passed through broken teeth,
Of the breach in the castle wall.
Even as a man who hearing her call,
Kneeled upon splinters of the fallen.
Bone - steel - wooden shields,
His heart held silent,
Eyes only seeing her pale smiling face.
Opening to the sound that whispered his name,
The call in the ancient song of stone.

A shiver that started in her grimy toes,
Flowing up as she heard.

While hands cruelly groped and tore,
Blood red ribbons,
Her garb almost fallen.
Filling her heart to find the memories,
She had always known,
Turning flesh into grey empty stone.

He knew - he smiled as water ran from eyes,
Making him rapidly blink.
Sending a shower of molten stone,
That blossomed as flowers.
Growing joining as they drifted down,
Silencing the helpless screams.
As Knights and Beast fell,
Under the weight of walls that grew,
From drops that knew their purpose.
To be a barrier that gives time,
So she can be saved - by the beat of her own heart,
For a man who had shared the secret of stone.

With a shake of her defiant head,
She reached and found the power.
Shattering the empty hearts,
That could never hold the soul.
Just the empty cravings of darkness,
A hunger worse than any beast.
Which could not stand as she made her way,
All falling as fresh cut wheat - so she could be.
With a heart that could hold her heart,
In a single beat - stronger then a measure of stone.

Silence descended,
No more screams.
Ships sailing away,
A few scattered survivors.
That knew that the King across the sea,
Would never have the body and soul,
Of a Princess who had fought with the strength of stone.

From him no sign,
Just an empty feeling.
As she despairing - searching among the bodies,
For any sign that he still lived.

ARC OF THE ANCIENTS

Wrapped clumsily her dress now no more than rags,
Her hair wild with eyes filling with hot tears.
No more anger just the fear of the price,
That she may pay for the love she craved.
From the man who had shown her his heart,
In every life that he brought forth.
To every cry of delight they had shone,
As they had walked - flown - crawled,
From the molten depth of stone.

Sun setting,
Dusk coming,
At the Wall she could not venture,
It had saved her.
But where was he?
Down the slope beyond the castle,
Brambles cut,
Rivulets flowing down bare bruised flesh.
Her feet bare to the cold muddy slope,
Sliding - tumbling landing by the waterfall of time.
To sit head in hands to weep,
Her heart crying,
Her body screaming.
Her soul dying,
To see once more the kind smile,
The hands that knew magic.
The Heart that made hers dance,
With no words spoken,
Just the Love shared.
When she saw him,
Needing no tools,
Carving with gentle fingers.
Helping dreams have life,
Beyond the world of stone.

If only she would look up,
She would see.
At the waterfall of time,
In the pool of dreams.
A hand breaking the surface,
Struggling to be free.
Of the world of stone,
That he had walked in to save her.

Not knowing that she sits,
In grief and weeps,
For the loss of her Stonecarver.[5]

-3-
SILENT LOVE

Within the silence of the cloud we dwell,
Soft hearts lying upon smooth round drops of rain.
To cushion our souls as we listen,
To the silence so mellow and watch the dawn at play.

Colours of a rainbow float warmly across the sky,
Thus the silent painter brings us the magic so profound
We watch as they melt in silence so far above the ground.
Touching us with empathy by a winds breath,
A sweet velvet kiss blossoming a flower within our breast.

Thus the silence is created from the perfume,
An aroma of graceful dance wafts by.
Our skin kissed alive by melting light,
Our hearts touch as we float.
Sharing the exotic brevity of one moment,
One beam of a petals smile.

Warm silent souls are we carried by the cloud,
Side by side just a kiss a away from touching.
Feeling this tranquillity of our minds.
Our eyes reflecting quiet pools of shimmering images,
In our silent dance we gaze into each other's eyes.

Floating into this dominion is the feeling of peace,
Shared contentment as we slowly fall into the colours
Savouring the silent rain upon our souls.
The mellow colour of sensual perfume,
Of flowers freshly bloomed within our eternal souls.

---

[5] *This poem has been soundscaped and is available direct from the Author as a MP3 file, a very haunting soundtrack!*

ARC OF THE ANCIENTS

Only in this silence can we freely fall,
Transformed as one.
Allowing the breeze to carry us away,
To a crimson horizon.
Waiting to feel the silence of Angels wings,
Thus we are changing once again.

Our hearts beating the rhythm,
Soaring upon the ripples of the sun.
Warming our silence at each stroke of our wings,
Turning in flight to touch our lips.
Gently caressing in a sensuous silent kiss,
Thus creating our heavenly fall.

Turning - holding - feeling,
Each silent beat our rainbow begins to play
The melody in the silence of today.
Metamorphosing kisses sparkling as we fall,
To earth as soft silver rain.

Beyond this dawn is heaven's gate,
Filling senses with an enchanted perfume.
That paints rainbows across a sensual sky,
On silver sand you can stand knowing the quickening.
A burning fire of new silence dwelling within,
Your magical soul reborn to enfold loves eternal grace.

Gaze upon the silver waters of a tranquil lake,
Forsake to articulate and hear within the silence
Two lovers who know they will never need to speak.
Of a silent love wished to be known for all,
This raptures journey within a lovers embrace.[6]

---

[6] *This poem has been soundscaped and is available direct from the Author as a MP3 file – a soft a gentle sound track!*

-4-
WINTER'S WATER-TIME

We are those that see the final wave,
A mighty ocean roar. From grey to white,
The sea can speak to followers of an ocean's warmth.
For awoken are the great spirits to follow the song,
To share the food for all that come.

It will be the mighty that choose to witness,
The final call. These are the generations,
From old to young to return to the beginning shore.
A curve of sand, a shallow reach of land that speaks,
Of those that tread the lonely walk.
So they may know we are here, in peace once more.

My song of death, the ripeness of an age,
For the rest I shall take upon that wind swept shore.
Those of family to come to stay,
To share my fluid sounds of joy as the stream,
Of my new ocean spills forth.

An echo of the one who knows,
I see as my brothers come to follow my eternal sleep.
She may only be a grey shadow to my winter's eye,
But my sound of wisdom finds the colour and flame,
Of her burning mind.

That song was sung as you danced amongst us,
So small and meek.
Fear not cousin, sister of time.
The joy is upon us as we reach,
To find the communion upon that beach.

For though you, as all on a winter's night,
Only know the world that doesn't sing.
Of one life, one love, one hope.
You dared to allow the fluid touch,
As we all lay waiting, watching as it flows,
From us to you our hope, our love, our eternal lives.

ARC OF THE ANCIENTS

You will hear our final song,
You will wonder why we stay ?
You will witness the youngest return to sing,
Of our final winter's day.

As I sing the fallen tone,
So that those that chose freely can follow.
To show the picture of our naked faith,
That now lie waiting within your reach.

From our place among the stars,
We watch the last flicker of life cease,
And wait awhile as the dawn now breaks,
Upon the dark winter beach,
The burden of the mighty are now at peace.

Shed no tear, bear no pain,
For the eleven songs that came,
So those that can be our witness,
That love from us to you,
Is the song you now can sing.

When those that come in winter's days,
 To follow, show them how to watch,
 How to wait, listen, then to find,
Then your help will open,
 Our communion of a winter's water time.[7]

---

[7] *This is the Fifth time this poem has been published. It was written for the 11 sperm whales that died on Sunday on the 8th of December 1994*

FAR TO THE RIGHT OF MAGIC POEMS

-1-
FAR TO THE RIGHT OF MAGIC

Between the pauses of reality's blend,
A hand reached out tapping me on the shoulder
With a voice that was surprising in clarity.
More than just a prayer of bells ringing to please,
But the lilt of a blarney stone well kissed.

A laughing angel with swan white wings,
Fluttering around inside my mind.
Or is the air blessed with the devil's charm,
With a chuckling shivering kiss
Keeping me there longer than I ever planned.

Always to remain a mystery this whisper,
Of a land far away in the heart of promises.
Never to be given in the seduction of tomorrow,
In the landscape deeper than a sigh
Of greener fields far to the right of magic.

This is but a moment in a busy day,
An idle wanderer caught in the light.
Closing eyes to savour a friendly chime,
A pearl polished by the grains of days
More than just a little grey.

-2-
CRIMSON TEARS

Upon your scales of emerald vermilion ebony I sit,
Fire veins stoking power of every muscle that you flex.
Making warm draughts of air from jewel tip wings,
That makes my heart bump and beat a rhythm
With every blink of your sapphire eyes we sing.

So like toys that Gods might scatter like a farm,
At the end of a dusty lane with a tractor no more than,
A child's whim that painted these colours from a map.
That an angel might send on a breath of wind,
To aid in the flight of a dragon's wing.

Creating whimsical clouds in a tinge of cherry,
Joining those that were never born from a dragons breath,
Ducking and diving over and in-between forests,
Scattering dozing sheep across saffron daisy fields
While hawk and dove rise to ponder our delightful scene.

Deepest red the horizon giving birth to twilight stars,
Becoming a blur in a slipstream of cool evening air
Taking my breath away as we burn streaks across the sky.
My eyes filling with tears as I cry out a greeting to those,
That waited long ago upon chalk white cliffs.

With gleeful delight you skim over hesitant heads,
Stareing in awe as your wings rise and twist.
Landing with no more than a puff or two in softest sigh,
Knowing the time has come to say goodbye
Can bring crimson tears to a dragon`s eye.

-3-
COLOURS OF A DREAM

My heart was a bird with a shattered wing,
Until I saw the beginning tapestry.
Locked away in your dark dusty attic,
Waiting for you to finally dare yourself
To be more than hope in a dream.

Shake the dust and cobwebs away,
Feel the power flow through your skin.
Then the colours will reach inside to,
Grow your heart to watch out for those that wait
In the land of a forgotton dream.

Let your soul dance beyond the boundary of your skin,
Feel the kiss of magic upon your lips
Let the rhythm give you new eyes.
With words you can really sing,
Then you will create a world beyond any dream.

Know that in your hand is a flame,
To melt a heart or make it sing.
As a beacon of light at the gate,
To welcome those that desire
To create new realities from a dream.

-4-

TOR

This is the beginning time in which I await,
Gazing out to watch the low mist.
Surround and devour the marshland below,
Among the silver lakes bordering the magic.
From which you advance leading those that witness,
The truth of legends being born.

You in shimmering velvet blue begin your ascent,
Among the wild flowers that make you into a perfume.
That makes men's heart melt to submit to your power,
Upon their knees they bow to honor and wait
The fire in your eyes to sacrifice their very lives.

On the red ochre trail that binds this place,
Your bare footsteps create the chimes that call
The birds from the sky and the beasts from the field.
With a canopy of downy white cloud that surrounds,
Only penetrated by the shaft of light that is your halo.
You look up and I know a goddess is more than a twinkle.
In your mischievous tawny eyes.

ARC OF THE ANCIENTS

By the final twist you are before me,
An owl hoots in welcome and I can't help the sigh.
As I smile turning as we raise our hands,
To salute the cheers rising from below.
As one we bless this Tor as a gateway,
For the coming magical dawn.

-5-
ATHENA

Sacred circle of crystal stone torch lit with many watchers,
From the shadow I walk cowled to the center
As I look up to the star lit sky I await the kiss of fire.
Thus within a moment the shaft of blue descends like quicksilver,
Engulfed and aflame I ascend to hear her.

No moment can be like this as I wait in the void,
Then I see her tall like a willow darkest night is her hair
Fire burns deep inside as she glides to my side.
With a shimmer two oak stools appear and we sit facing each other,
There is laughter in every movement and grace beyond compare.

She is the voice of the sword and balm of the heart,
The scales of her justice embrace me.
Her breath sweeter than heaven,
As she opens me to see the brevity of this night
To feel the flames that teaches that this was my beginning.

Like a bird taking its first flight she opened my eyes,
To know that our whispers can reach the silent time.
Like two conspirators we laughed with joy as all can be manifest,
Then within the blink of an eye she held my hands in hers
Filling my heart with a breathless promise........

-6-
MAGIC ISLE

Verdant hills in gentle curve to the tranquil sea,
Above a sky that is rich in cerulean blue.
With clouds that scurry when the wind is a kiss,
In wings of the free that always need
A perch to rest singing of this land of bliss.

To walk is to be held in your arms,
Feeling the comfort of your bouquet.
That speaks of sea and sand,
With flowers in bloom so wild and fair
Making my heart stop and stare.

Would any believe that you reside,
On this little planet called earth.
Among the isles of the north,
That welcomes those that hear the songs
Of sea sky and land.

You will always be with me on any path,
I care to walk in sun or snow.
In any time that I choose I know that this fair jewel,
Is the center heart beyond time.
Giving freely your sense of hope,
In a breath deep within a magic Isle.

-7-
NO SHADOW FALLS

They became reflections of tears in our eyes,
As Angels with gossmer wings destined to fly.
To no longer be treated like a lost summer,
By hands that only kissed with anger
When a world turns a blind eye.

34

ARC OF THE ANCIENTS

So a journey to another land I would like to see,
I invite you to trace the path that is hope to be...

Footsteps across the rainbow is the first sign,
Breaking through the mist so benign.
For fire wings that descend to the trees,
Crowning the light that signals the approaching
Dance of the music of time.

Three children gather heart flowers in the valley,
Soaring whispers weave and dive.
To play the laughter of kindness to deliver,
A promise made among the stars
To show that magic is a child`s heart.

The symphony of rainbow light pours down sparkling,
On gossamer wings they witness a smile.
Innocent awe as they gather more than joy,
Reaching with tiny hands to weave
Heart flowers into a multidimensional dream.

Then the fairy folk soar with a blanket of colour in dream,
Stretching day into night as they play under starlight.
A kind moon as witness to children`s laughter as they see,
A gateway in the arms of a lily on a pale green lake
To see a land that smiles so no-shadow- falls.....[8]

---

[8] On Damiola, Anna, and the one with no-name who represents those never seen in the public
eye.....

-8-

PURPLE PASSION

A forest of leaves cloak you,
A purple sky opened to beckon the rain.
That cools your hot skin to be viewed,
Shining as you dance within grace.
Imprinting a vision that does not deceive,
Making the world seek to embrace.

Your heart beats the passion of the wild,
Turning rain to mist as you leap.
To gather in your arms that which keeps,
The fires burning and never sleeps.
Among oak ash willow that sway,
In every breath in time you take.

I came at your call to see the fairy dance,
To hear your heart purr.
Melting in the golden glow of a moon of honey,
That gladdens me that you are free.
To pursue your dance within me,
Crying as you see the mystery of the purple passion.

-9-

ETERNAL KISS

I was only walking past lost in thought,
When you whispered to me.
An echo lost in the wind,
This haunting call from an age long past
Opening the doorway with your perfumed kiss.

You stopped me, so I turned onto a path,
In a forgotten land of gray chipped stones
Until my feet came to rest at a granite obelisk.
My heart gripped waiting for you to be,
More then just a scent captivated by a breeze.

ARC OF THE ANCIENTS

Every vibration strained to catch a glimpse,
Of this hallowed lady of a lost land.
Frozen with white knuckles,
 Holding onto grey granite stone.
Waiting and waiting,
To never see but a kiss
Lingering like warm mist.
That could only fade as the sun rose,
To a day that is not yesterday's bliss.

Your call was so strong I saw you in today,
On this path among these lost stones.
As in a dream you would dance into my arms,
Feeling your lips in an eternal kiss.

But through sun sparkling tears I saw the awful truth,
My heart falling.
As I whisper your name,

Etched deep into the stone before me...[9]

-10-
THE CUP

I am thirsty I see in the pale moon light,
Reflecting within every curve and lip.
Cool to touch in each tastebud that sparkles,
Awakening memory upon a day that is a sip
Never taken but given in flame.

---

[9] For Rachel

37

Unremarkable to some as they see no heaven,
No shine as they hold you with no eyes.
To wonder as they touch the bead of rainbow light,
Glistening upon your side the nectar you give
Without hesitation to reveal the dust of their lost sight.

Passing liquid colour from hand to dry hand,
 Trickling away through fingers that cannot grasp.
A side that is not a reflection of their own,
Haunted feeling of a memory that they once sipped
From this eternal magical source.

Within wind rain and mist you came,
Offering me a mystery in a thirst quenching sip.
Awakening my heart to a landscape of new possibilities,
Knowing that I would give more than take
So a trickle will become a flood.

-11-
WOLFEN HEART

Born from the feral and free,
In dark shadow dream in blood red haze
Among the contorted trunks of moss laden trees.
Swift along deer trodden paths in early morning mist,
That cover and shroud the sleek hunger
That is an echo of a wolfen heart.

Hidden from the curious is the entrance of a cave,
Where beyond are golden eyes staring out to watch those
That stumble across the boundary of his home and hearth.
To commune with the power of teeth that can rent,
The warm blood filled flesh of the foolish kind
Becoming the sacrifice for a wolfen heart.

ARC OF THE ANCIENTS

When moon is full to bursting in the velvet dark,
The shadows are alive with the soft pad of paws
In a forest holding its breath as the silence is broken.
By the haunting music of the howling time,
That reaches deep to chill the soul or let a spirit be free
This is the season to listen to the beat of a wolfen heart.

Those that rise to the challenge will be forever changed,
When the mystery of the wild becomes a siren voice
That draws the souls of those that dare to venture.
Beyond the safety of their known lands,
To surrender the fear deep and see the truth
In the way of a wolfen heart.

12-
WINTER SNOW

I am dying for the love of you is the way of a life,
That bleeds all over my soul as a deep red tapestry.
That I will leave this mortal coil in despair,
 For the dream that was not to be.
Crying that I cannot shine in the light when darkness is all around,
Leaving me breathless and cold I deliver my soul unto you
All that I am will fade away in the cold winter`s snow.

I cry the blood of my heart into the silence of the coldest night,
As all those that leave to go beyond the veil
Leaving a shadow is all that I shall be in the final cycle of reason.
The symbol of love is my heart calling out for those that can be,
To See the lives that are just feelings in stone
To a cry of the wolf that becomes silent in the cold winter snow.

Then the stillness is a reality that blows,
Like a wind that shatters the soul.
Leaving me naked alone bereft of hope laid before you in cruel repose,

So all shall feed upon the one that hoped loved and died for thee.
When the blood fades into cool blue snow lift your head and see,
That in heaven there will be the flowering
 Of a night that has no darkness.
In Divinity of you in the howl of the wolf,
 Of your eternal heart of soul.

-13-
TO PLAY THE DREAM

No longer just a ride into the unknown,
Where every shadow is a surprise
But a world to embrace and refine.
In colour of spirit and complex mind,
To shape the landscape for any time.

To play the dimension like soft bread dough,
Orchestrating the elements is your mission
In choosing every colour shape and vision.
To seize the choice that can breathe,
New life is your glorious decision.

Banishing fears that have no place,
In your inner realm is the beauty
That is yours to savour in any harbour.
You choose to be or allow mystery,
To take you beyond the limits of me.

To know that this rhapsodic song is free,
To choose any beginning that is the light
Of your guide to breathe the purple kind.
Is your magical key to unlock the doors,
Of a lucid dimensional play beyond dream.

-14-
GIANT'S LAMENT

Grey eyes ringed dark in seeking desperation,
With tumulus clouds moping a brow of chestnut hair.
Ice cold rivulets running down sunburnt cheeks,
With an oak tree for a pick between a broken smile
Is a tower of flesh and bone in a child bereft of any hope.

Remembering a bright morning a chance to pick flowers,
A gift for his darling mother down the mountain path.
Running swiftly past the scary black shadow of pumice and shale,
Into the warm green kissed valleys full of bright colours
By crystal lagoons where he became terrified by a vision.

A thousand walks over miles that should be known,
Turning to grief when a giant runs afraid
From the fear inside a heart that can break any rock or stone.
Twisting in circle after circle dizzy and ready to burst,
Into tears that can drown any little folk who point and stare.

Until by a hot desert never lashed by rain or an ocean wave,
In torn brown clothes he cries and washes away
A thousand nesting birds who shouldn`t have stayed.
But Taken wing when a giant weeps his anguish,
Turning a desert into a sea of lonely tears.

A RAINBOW OF LOVE POEMS

-1-

FALLING ANGEL

When the earth is too heavy it is the colour I see,
Falling so deep that an ocean can never catch me.
So long that a prayer becomes an eternity,
I feel your breath upon my skin.
I can be seen as a man who is no longer a shadow,
Who knows that your eyes are the fires of heaven?

When vision of reality is twined with your kiss,
The softness that lingers upon our lips.
I no longer need heaven but to be an embrace,
Wrapped in your arms forever is the dream
That your heart will always call to me.

Leaving eternity is just a wish,
Unless your heart invites me to be more
Then all the stars that shine.
For a universe that is waiting for me,
To break all the rules that is your kiss.

Can I feel the touch that is more than I can imagine,
Will I be lonely beyond the grasp of reality?
Can I cry so my tears do not fall on the desert?
That is a world that no longer believes in the heart,
Of magic that is held within in a woman's smile.

All I have is journey that lasts until you say,
That I can be more than the shadow that you wish.
For all the space that is between us,
I have a heart that only lives to feel you close.
So I can sleep no longer alone in the barren waste,
Of life's eternal dream.

I am but a falling angel that is dying to grasp,
The moment that passion stirs the fires that
Turn the heavens star fire into a glance.
From your eyes that make me fall to my knees,
So I can see you as you really are.

To drink from the ambrosia that makes,
One picture of one time of one soul
Making you into the flesh and blood that I can hold.

-2-
THE DANCE OF SOULS

Feeling you step closer - wrapped in fire,
Reaching with heart for the music clearer than sound
Faster than colour in the choices of mind.
This I speak crossing the boundary of a wish,
More subtle then a dream and the desire of a kiss.

Enticing and teasing the whisper - wrapped in fire,
Trembling with open soul the feelings upon an open palm
Travelling beyond sight to take the step off a lonely cliff.
Falling to pass through the mantle and the pressure of an age,
To fly without wings to the place centre left of a star.

A beckoning mischievous wink - wrapped in fire,
In the suggestion of fingers tickling the chin of a sleeping god.
You dance with colours manifest in a rainbow,
A feeling taking the tears of a heart with a smile broader
Then any pattern painted as a constellation.

Unashamedly wanton a purr - wrapped in fire,
More naked then unclothed flesh - unlocking worlds
Once hidden so deep, spring fresh and alive.
To be born in the laughter of light as our star bodies twine,
Slipping sliding into you and I is more than a kiss.

Breathing each other in - wrapped in fire,
Slowly each layer is stripped away with gentleness
Going deeper and deeper guided by the desire to know.
To touch the face that is kept hidden from the world of grey,
To be unafraid in the freedom we hunger to express.

As one we breathe out - wrapped in fire,
You and I know the beat that our hearts dream.
We are more than just the scattering of light created flesh,
And the world we share grew flowers that we have to tend
Keeping us apart but we know the dance of souls...

-3-

IN THE RAIN...

Naked to feel the caress in elixir light,
On a hillside open to a sapphire dawn.
Is a soul who feels the first drop,
To kiss her skin in the inaugural step
In this exhilarating spring dance.

Streaming in rivers that splashes in surges,
From her head to wet dancing toes.
Making skin a satiny touch of glowing passion,
From vibrations that massage
Her aches and pains into sweet oblivion.

In every droplet is a beat that makes,
Every breath a gasp that opens.
Her heart to a flight of ascending joy,
Reaching a crescendo that makes every pore cry
In harmony to the morning stars.

In open naked glistening fire she,
Embraces nature's giving heart.
Becoming the liquid soul of heaven,
Pouring inhibitions away to dance
Forever rapturous grace in awe.

44

-4-
MISSING YOU IN TIME

There was a time that said your name,
Whispering softly in my ear.
Making my heart ache with a smile,
From here to the time I would see you again.

Now the years have flown since we said our last goodbye,
Time no longer serves me more than to say.
That I can no longer have time with you,
But the yearning doesn't stop just because time tells me to.

Our time was always brief only a handful of days,
In a score of years but the look in your eyes
Will have to last me while I wait to see if,
This pale blue planet will turn to favour us one more time.

The years pass with no more words,
Lost without your wicked beguiling smile.
Barren without the hope to be warm once more in your heart,
To give life to the promise that we would bridge the gap in our time.

Time told me to let you go to let you remain a memory,
Long cherished for the time you chose to share with me.
Then the cracks appear announcing that I cannot live,
With out you in my heart my life missing you in time.

-5-
I HAD A DREAM...

I had a dream about you
You were so lovely,
I almost died.
But I hugged you instead,

and wallowed in the smell of you.
Your eyes shone,
I couldn't stop looking into you.
I almost died
But I kissed you instead,
and you kissed me back.
I was so surprised,
I had never been kissed before.
You grinned,
I almost died
But I held your hand instead,
And we waited for the number seven bus.
Which unfortunately hit the kerb and ran us over,
oops.
So we died.
But we never let go,
They found our hands
Like a heart,
They cried....

-6-

DOORWAY

Breathing so deep as I hold on to you,
Wanting to step through and embrace
Seeing that you frame a world.
That is more than just a wish,
But a promise of grace.

Fascination in your strength is a mellow,
Sigh that billows and blows the cobwebs away.
Your glory stands in every line and curve,
Of jewel encrustation in every quirk
That you are salvation as I lurch.

ARC OF THE ANCIENTS

Emotions are running high in the face,
That you present to me in every polished line.
Is the faith I feel as I open you,
To feel the warm breath of promise
As I fly through to your land of milk and honey.

Rolling down moss coloured fields,
Dizzy with delight as I feel the sunshine
Of welcome as I stop and see.
My world made new in every possibility,
By closing the door on any doubt that I could reach.

-7-
FAITH

Faith is when your soul,
Tells your heart that you don`t mind.
A commitment that will carry you,
On wings to the other side
Of any yawning chasm that you find.

A time of conviction in a field of doubt,
Scattered with the mines of evasion.
That flutters in your heart,
Trembling your stride until the silence calls
And you know the faith in which you walk.

Faith is when your palpitation,
Is a harmony that the universe replies
Bringing a wave of light.
That will shine and keep you warm,
In the cold frost of those that fear and fawn.

To bear witness for those who search,
Grey shadows to entomb fear and antipathy
And become the light that can be.
A portent that they deliberate,
On pathways to a faith unseen.

-8-

SAND KISS

Upon a beach with a roar of sound,
You came to rest in a wave that polishes
To shine and shimmer a morning not bound.
In the heat of a sun you became a jewel,
To lay beside me and rest upon my cheek.

The ocean knows your grace as you move,
Upon this shining globe of blue and green.
To mesmerise those that find you,
To build castles that deliver a sky
Of planets and moons that you reside.

The surf delivered me unto you,
To allow a moment that is a rainbow.
Becoming a deep caress upon my soul,
As I know that pattern in sand
Is a memory of long ago.

Just a grain to some but you know an eternal truth,
That beckons me to raise you to shine in my eyes.
To dazzle in refraction as I hold cupped in my heart,
Your magic that opens the way for you to be
More than just a kiss in the sand.

-9-

UNICORN DANCE

From the volcano he hears her gracious call,
Through incandescent rain to the pine forest below,
Hooves on fire as he leaps and prances,
Raising ivory twisted horn to be his flute in tune,
Causing his mane of turquoise to dance and cavort.

Among purple star flowers she shakes her flank,
Setting silver tears to spin and fly,
With a flare of her nostrils she scents,
An exaltation wrapped in the chord an answer,
Of her wish in every measure of his heart.

Deep brown eyes alight to a morning glade,
On the edge a vision of capering love,
In spring and vault in a sea of purple flowers,
She cuts a swathe making the air flash as horn,
Vibrating spirit in flesh to be born.

Tails twisting in a blur of glistening flanks,
Heaving and rising up with a clash of horn,
Two chords mixing to produce a melody,
That makes blue eyes lock with brown,
In white foam of a unicorn dance.

-10-
SHIELD OF LOVE

I walk among the despondent,
The scavengers with faded soul.
In the land of cruel crimson scars,
Who bear swords that cannot cut
The heart that radiates a shield of love.

Everything that is swayed knows,
A power that can withstand any
Attack from the tremulous that skulk.
In cloaks of night that have no hope,
But to observe the love that shields.

Turning dark into coloured light,
So they can feel the heat waves
That can flame the ache away.
Evaporating sorrow that came to stay,
As souls feel love as their shield.

This is not to stay apart in heart,
But to rejoice in the compassion
Of invocation as loves fills the soul.
Breaking down barriers so all,
Can share as one in the loving shield.

THE OTHERSIDE OF MIDNIGHT POEMS
-1-
BETWEEN HEART BEATS

The silence of a rock bearing down squeezing the space,
Existing to tear muscle from bone creating the
Final flower to arch its stem to breathe of heaven.
Until the crush of petals stain aching flesh until emotions
Breach the ocean like a whale in hunted throes of pain.

No gentle tears falling but those armed with flamethrowers,
That scorch and blaze their way to scar the landscape so even
Mighty oaks whimper as they crackle, burn and fall to ash.
With colours bleeding away to pale tones of empty grey,
Making the pendulum wait for the sound of the next heartbeat.

In the silence pictures of faces, of times, and of hope
Falling to smash into pieces against the brick wall,
When the world is caught on a crimson wave.
Flying into the sun where there is no place to run,
To hide, but to be the torch that will burn and burn.

No more air just a purple dream to stoke the fear,
In a grotesque grin frozen on clowns in red hats choking
Babies with dummies until you are fit to burst and scream!
Not the cold sweaty fish with glazing eyes waiting for
The knife to descend and chop and chop,
So you know your heart is beating again.

The temperature drops and you fall into the arms of
Walking flowers, with petals that caress slivers of ice.
Bringing winter to the places that ache for the warmth
Of summer instead of this new world of purple and blue,
Waiting for lightning to strike and shatter this crystal tomb.

In the silence no more pain, no more heavy earth bound flesh,
Only the lifting of all the laws until you are free to rise and fly.
Slowly ascending until like a rocket you become more than
Thought, more than light, beyond feeling but a concept,
An idea greater than a dream and more real than reality.

Then you see...
Wrapped in joy...
Cascading in Love...
The -

To never know because your heart chose that moment to beat.
Returned to lay in sorrow and weep...
Yearning to return to the place between heart beats.

-2-

ALIEN COMMINGLED

Witness the petals to fall on deaf eyes,
Blind ears with feeling mouth of talkative skin.
Is a blue sky full of wisdom empty in contemplation?
In the tears of the swallow that fly in confusion.
As soul feathers make their ascent,
Flowering a gateway to rich and healthy lives
Wearing colours upon their skin.

As Whales hope in the fruitless charm of man,
So the elephant travels to make the call
Of wild and abandoned times in the darkest mine.
Where ants follow more than just orders,
Like Penguins diving in splashes.
Making the waves flow as sweet maiden breath,
Into paintings of old men sitting on trains full to the brim
Happy smiles linked like coiled naked snakeskin.

Upon a tableau of wind in rain of sun and snow,
Heaped together like mussels and cockles
With a starfish pointing the way for everything to begin again.
Across the realms of purple twilight stars,
Casting more light then shadow over the canals of Mars.

-3-
COLD LULLABY

From the very core of my being,
I feel the seductive lullaby.
Caressing my bones until they ache,
Making each breathe a lover`s sigh
In a terrible haunting parody that breaks.

My heart is a trembling butterfly,
Attempting in tired rhythm to find
An escape from the blue white taste.
That is numbing flesh in the promise,
Laid by the comfort of crystal stars.

In mesmerising dance that distracts me,
Convincing my eyelids to close.
To allow all to withdraw in the arms,
That maintain a welcome to stay
In a yawn that vibrates a world at bay.

That holds no enhanced colours to interest,
Just the focus of somebody yearning
To discard the weight of frozen chicken flesh.
Caught upon a tableau until the blade sweeps,
In the cut of the coldest scythe.

-4-
HOLOCAUST

When anger and hatred is poured into the empty vessels,
Of those easily marked with a star or a ring.
The stamp of difference is a curse to be burnt,
Becoming the playground of those never to learn.

Marble statues so cold in bereft of a prayer,
When humanity is ashes upon the tongue.
No beauty in lives made into furniture,
Broken up as firewood to chill your heart.

Under the gray skies full of shadow,
An Angel with ash-coated wings kneels in despair.
Where no one can breathe is a memory never to be forgotten,
In nightmares of lives lost across the landscape of time.

We are not bread to be baked in ovens,
Or a carcass to be butchered in mud covered huts.
Or wheat to be harvested in blood soaked fields,
Or our spirits to be tortured in the name of religion.

In every country across this world the killing fields,
Have scars that still fester and burn.
Of the injustice of humanity's unforgiven,
That makes the word of the people say no more!

-5-
MAKING PLANETS

One thought is a beginning as you shape,
The cosmic scheme to gather into being
A little stardust with a temperate breathe.
Lighting an atom fire that bonds them together,
So they learn to dance and entertain.

Takes a little expectorate to polish fiery matter,
Keeping them molding holding and folding
Making sure that finger tips are kept at bay.
While a breeze will be enough to cool the metal heart.
As you wait for the crust to form and not fade.

Invent a cosmic clock and allow time to do its work,
Remembering to set an alarm as over cooked
Is not the best way to start this kind of day.
When a planet overheats and explodes in your face,
You will have to start all over again.

A eon or two will pass as you wait,
Then give it a good lick to settle all the land
Grabbing a few passing comets letting them be.
Fiery ice no more but an ocean or two,
So when you sneeze a little life can see
A place to do all their naughty little deeds.

-6-

POCKETS FULL OF SAND

Pockets full of sand makes sense in away,
When I feel things slipping away
Time like water all soaked away.
Absorbing is this moment taking attention away,
Despairing in a funny dream like way.

If I scream will they all go away,
Can I say that I'm tired of their selfish ways?
Can someone help me find away,
Will there be a revolution so there will be more
Than sand in my pockets or should I pour it all away.

Living in a room which is now full of sand,
Is kind of Egyptian in very odd way.
Like a mummy with its guts in tan pottery jars,
I think that is very suffocating wouldn't you agree?
Maybe even funny in a crazy hysterical sort of way.

Are you paying attention to me?
Are my words just sand dribbling away.
But then I thought I heard an angel once,
But that was sand in the wind wasn't it
Blowing me away to fill a vacant pocket is not mad is it?

-7-

JUST MAD

Falling in a tumble through a gate,
To a land most bizarre
I could almost wish I was late.
Where trees wore faces so strange,
When they smiled they looked quite deranged.

A gingerbread cat fell from the sky,
Bounced twice and landed in a pie
Splashing a penguin who couldn`t die.
Until the mushrooms had finished playing,
With a big green baboon who said slay em.

Bees flew with chocolate elephant ears,
So peculiar that honey tasted really odd.
When covered in great big bunnies,
That hopped upside down wearing
Yellow pinafores over their tummies.

I had a dance with a kangaroo,
So big that stars fell out of its ears
Making a frightful hubbaloo.
Scaring mice who were driving,
Gazelle so untidy that hamsters
Arrested them for speeding! [10]

-8-

THE LAMENTING CORPSE

Tis annoying laying here in the gutter,
When people so carelessly ignore me
Side stepping their shoes around me.
Is it because there are too many colours?
Do my discharging odours offend you?

Tis annoying laying here in the gutter,
When people throw up all over me
Side swiped by your holy vehicles.
Is it because those rats feed on my flesh?
Does my decaying smile upset you?

---

[10] *For my Daughter Cassie!*

ARC OF THE ANCIENTS

Tis annoying laying here in the gutter,
When people stand moaning above me
Side slipping in my green ooze like flesh.
Is it because pigeons shit on my head?
Do my rotting soft tissue's bore you?

Tis annoying laying here in the gutter,
When people idly kick me in head
Sideways glancing into my cavernous chest.
Is it because children play with my eyes?
Does my suit need dry cleaning?

-9-

RIDING THE PALE HORSE

If you wish to surrender the names of those that are lost to oblivion,
Marking the world with temperate dreams is the place of a thousand
pavilions.
Each colour is a flag of stars drifting on the breath of a goddess,
Waving goodbye to the children who ride on the back of a pale horse.

A million trumpets herald the opening of the gates to a world long dead,
Containing the face that winks through the dust of a storm waiting to be
fed.
A picture sent back that broke the minds of those that choose to deny,
The fact that they will not be the first to see the shadow of the pale horse.

If you wish to surrender the idea that you cannot know the children,
That stepped in the red dust before you bequeathing the N' building.
Opening your mind to the truth that you were never alone in space,
Then one day you will follow in the footsteps of the pale horse.

A million flowers blossomed on a future day of a world longing to live,
When the dry ice melted and the red earth breathed you a gift.
That those long forgotten will show that you do know the texture that is waiting,
To impress its legacy that your blood flows in the heart of the pale horse.

If you wish to surrender the pride that you were the first to know,
Marking the world with the colour of your paintings in a thousand lost bows.
No arrow can reach the point when you cannot accept the destination,
That is waiting to carry you beyond the stars on the back of a pale horse.

-10-
RUMINATIONS OF VOMIT

You left me to lie here, all helpless and cold,
When I could be warm and safe travelling.
Through your slipways and byways,
Getting to know your intestinal tract.

To be absorbed into your blood,
To be part of you until you become dust.
But you threw me away you bastard,
Because of your gastronomic lust.

Don't just sit there with glacier eyes,
I'm here waiting for you to realise.
That you could scoop me up,
Returning me to your handsome guts.

Now I'm congealing all over your clothes,
I'll stink the place out
While you gawp and moan.

Don't I look appetising any more?
Look, get a plate, knife and fork,
And I bet you will say give me more!

Hey you have gone all red, purple and blue!
Was it something I said?
No please, don't gag, its just a reflex too…

ARC OF THE ANCIENTS

Oh charming, now you writhe and moan,
Don't bother thrashing and crashing
You do have enough storage space you know!

Come on don't be a baby,
Just open wide and let me slide back inside.

Making your tongue swell all purple like that,
Isn't going to help, please just relax.

Oh but now you've gone all quiet and blue,
Pissed yourself and spoilt the view.

Oh great!
Gatecrashers flying into plagiarise.

To be eaten and vomited all over again!

Always knew flies had terrible table manners.

-11-
I. D.I.O.T.

It came as no surprise that the call finally came,
Didn't they realise to pass up such an oppurnity was
Incapable of being in existence on a world full
Of the possibilities that can only come from facing,
The fact they were in charge of the fates now decreed.

Ilogical would be the word that captain's hear in their,
Dome like ears as all the ships changed course to the
Insanity that waited on a small world in the corner
Of a spiral armed galaxy in a time far far away,
That could only be concluded was facing the wrong way.

In the afternoon at tea time they all arrived,
Deciding that all the ships would hide behind a moon.
Incase the native's of the planet below turned thier tv's,
Over and realised that their planet was surrounded by
Those that saw the possibilities of a world that voted in shrubs and trees.

In case you are wondering what happened next,
Don't worry as all will become clear as you look
Inside the contents of the box before you.
Or so they told me as I pointed out,
That the straps were too tight as those above roared this can't be!

Incredibly the ships with captain's with dome like ears,
Didn't know what to make of it when those whispers of
Ilogical you mad bastards don't you see.
Orders are one thing but we'll never to finish our tea!
This is our fate if we have deal with a bloody shrubbery!

-12-
WALKING IN MY BLOOD

Why did you crack open my chest?
Am I a crab, the seafood on your table?
You took my heart and squeezed it dry,
Did you enjoy slipping your tongue deep inside?
Your face all red with the guilt as you fed.
Because you know that this is the beginning,
The taste that maybe tangy but its still a walk in my blood.

I felt your teeth tug and rip; I saw your pleasure,
Your hunger as you slurped your way through all that blood.
So why did you avis irate me while I slept?
You know it will be hard for me to take a breath,
If you keep those lungs preserved in jars on your bedside chest.
You better be careful not to open them for they keep,
My last breath waiting to burst,
So foul it will dam you for walking in my blood.

ARC OF THE ANCIENTS

Will you take some onions and fry?
My liver in red wine sauce, with a side portion of kidney,
And some hot fat chips with my boiled eyes?
Come on you said you were my friend,
But you didn't hesitate to take that knife,
Taking away my life so you can walk away in my blood.

You can make ropes from my intestines,
But where will you climb?
No matter how high the mountain is, you will
Always smell the hot sweet iron flavour upon your skin.
You will always be walking in my blood.

What will you do with the rest?
Will you make chairs from my leg bones?
Will my skin cover the books?
That you read by a lusciously familiar shaped lampshade,
That will cast blood red shadows,
Reminding you that you butchered your dearest friend.
Even as you tan the leather for the shoes,
That will mark you as the one who walks in my blood.

You stir your soup with my scapula,
Cut flesh with my sharpened finger bones,
Can you not see the mistake in consuming me?
I don't suppose you saw my tears fall,
Ah I understand you drank those too.
Oh dear one there is a price for stealing,
The one who could have freed you,
From your desire to walk in my blood.

Do you know I can hear you?
Those ears still work attached to my head,
With torn and empty eye sockets I may be blind.
But I know as I take my rest,
Waiting for you to take your pleasure,
To dip your spoon into the soft folds of my brain,
To taste the thoughts, memories, and feelings,
Of the one you are dining upon.
That you can never escape from me,
Forever my friend you will walk in my blood.

61

Next time you should have taken out my tongue!
Oooh I can hear you sharpening a knife,
I can feel your breath as you open my mouth,
Oh you. Fu -mmmmffmmmfufuufmmm.
Oou are a otten ar-urd an I ill ay oou alk ii y ood![11]

-13-
KYRIE ELEISON

Falling to my knees as an autumn leaf,
Everything languid in the strata of my mind.
Trying my best to hold my heart together,
Even as I know everything is falling by design.

I am scattered upon a tempest wind,
Rainbows torn apart to splatter the sky.
Each one a jewel of colour becoming a grain,
Of sand to hurt my tortured eyes.

I lived in hope but times cruel sloth,
Made my heart abandon measured beats.
Ripping the fabric of vision in a bloody blur,
Of medusa's unforgiving conceit.

Everything slows down to stone,
Chilling the reason to utter the only word.
To break me free that is the sword,
That wounds deeper than any lie.

I know I shall witness the dying time,
All I ask that I don't carry the burden alone.
To listen to my desperate cry,
Even one hug can shatter a heart in stone!

---

[11]Translation! *Oh you are a rotten bastard! And I still say you walk in my blood!!*

-14-
DARK CLOCK

All they hear in shadow is a tick,
The chime of the darkest night
In the grey walls of the lost.
A murmur a gasp a sigh that wait,
For the door of light that is tock.

In cloaks that are the eddies of those that watch,
Like butterflies wrapped in amber
Wanting the release so no more tick.
Can haunt the hearts of a slowing clock,
Winding slowly down to stop.

Masks for those that wander and weave,
That have become reflection to those that lie
Prone in helpless frozen time.
Walking talking along the border line,
On faces turned away from tick or tock.

To give is to cross from the shadow time,
Embracing those that wait in pain
To share the tears and hearts and minds.
Without questions or demands but to join,
And allow them the dignity to say
Stop that blasted clock! [12]

---

[12] In Memory of Barbara

-15-
"IT'S ALMOST TIME TO GO HOME"

Did I hear it right?
Did you say what I thought you said?
Can I believe the picture you describe?
Can I believe that you are killing my time?

Why is everything frozen?
Why do I feel so cold?
Why are you really here?
Why did you have to say its time?

Your words have become a mantra,
They slip from my lips as I close my eyes
Will this be for the very last time?
The pillow is soft but your words are a neon sign.

I know my sleep becomes longer every day,
Time slipping away to materialize as a dark cloak.
Even as the light fades I see the glint of a scythe,
Even as you say soon it will be that time.

So do I rush around and scream that I know?
Or do I hasten to finish the work that I have begun?
So do I walk talk and just breathe one day at a time?
Turning your words into a dreamtime darkened sun.

I shiver as everything is held,
Can I tremble a little?
Shake and stomp and just cry,
Until I stop - closing my eyes.

To observe where I started and recognize where I had begun.

I hold onto the memories that are paintings,
Hanging in my gallery under a wreath of smiles.
Even as it begun with a cry and a journey of tears,
When I prayed for my summer time under a joyful sun.

ARC OF THE ANCIENTS

I live in hope like the chalice cup that I know,
Exists in every heart and I do my best to share.
The song of a dream that brings a light,
To the lips to quench a little thirst that says I care.

It's like any day but my fingers grow numb,
The song has only a little time to be sung.
But the hope grows deeper in the feeling,
In the love that is waiting for me
On the other side of a mirror warped sun.

Clarity is when you know that you a hold a key,
To the gateway that is waiting
In the right hand corner of a field
Magically laid out upon a tartan cloth.
Under the purple sky with molten silver of three moons,
At the dusk of a strangely familiar orange and red alien sun.

My first memory slams back into me,
Wrapping me in the arms that gave me the key.
And is waiting for me like an angel with a heart that knows,
That its time to let go.
Even as I try to hold on,
Resisting the call that says
"It's almost time to go home - soon my son."

-16-
FUNERAL OF LILLY & THEN CHO

This afternoon we laid Lilly to rest,
She had been lying in state for three days.
We had to wait for the high winds to die down,
This afternoon the calm came so we could now bury her at last.

The coffin was small; she was laid on azure cloth with a little pillow,
Her name on the cardboard coffin lid plain to see.
The Pine wooden sides polished and clean,
Didn't have a pine lid for Lilly
But I don't think she will mind.

My daughter prepared the flowers, all small but bright,
She was sad but calm now and very solemn.
She was very close to her friend and had shed her tears,
But she was ready to lay her friend to rest.

I had the honor of helping to carry the coffin,
To the graveside with its dark black earth waiting
Under the gray twilight sky I hummed a tune.
For some reason the national anthem but then,
It always sounded like a funeral march to me.

The coffin was so light it could have been empty,
But little Lilly was long gone and only her tiny shell remained.
Very gently she was lowered into the ground,
My daughter encouraging me to say a few words.

"You were a friend to my daughter,
With love we say farewell.
Under the stars of the cosmos you will lay,
Never to be forgotten."

It was dignifying and moving as we took turns scattering,
The first hand falls of earth.
Then helped to fill the grave until the blanket was covering,
Lilly's last resting place.

My daughter is happy that we have done well for her friend,
A stone marker will be show the place.
And with her cuddled close we left the graveside,
To the warmth of home.

For Lilly
R.I.P.
Born July 12th 2000 - Died January 21st 2001
The kindest Orangest Guinea pig I've known.

But then on that same night
Went our dear Cho...

You knew Lilly couldn't go alone,
You missed her as much as we.
But you were her bigger sis,
And you wanted to make sure

That littly Lilly wouldn't have to take
The journey to heaven's gate
All on her own....

Cho
R.I.P.
12/7/00 - 23/1/01

-17-
DOLPHIN KIND

We all dream of another voice in the darkness,
To feel no longer alone in the playground of space.
To know that we can reach out to a heart,
That knows that we too want to dance
The call of our hearts among the stars in daring grace.

They are here beside us waiting,
For us to acknowledge that they breathe
The same colours that we deny.
To conceive that they are already here,
That we can share in the waters of their time.

With their song is a promise of glory,
A melody of sound to cross the distance.
To bring joy that is more than just a plea,
That no distance will divide a dolphin`s
Call to live in our oceans heart in peace.

They are a rhythm of a future,
A transparency of colour in every wave.
That belongs to every soul who hears their call,
With love to turn cold hearts to warmth
So all can sing with one soul that never falls.

Through time and stars they came,
But will we awake to share this gift
Making a home which is more than bliss.
To feel their hope that we can face,
The truth of a race we know as dolphin kind.[13]

---

[13] EXPANSION OF THE INTRODUCTION POEM IN THE NOVEL *EXODUS: THE DOLPH/IN SAGA*

-18-
A RIPPLE IN FOCUS

In the sky a blend of colour that makes me shiver,
Like ice that makes more than a pattern to the sea.
Dwelling deep in the sound of a whale breaching,
Cascading emerald white foam in bubbling mirth
Of shining eyes that my daughter gives freely.

Is a whirlwind that is breathless in height,
From a mountain top that talks of the future.
Weaving us to dance with tranquil threads of blue,
To touch a silky breathe of perfume in orange clouds.

Shaping a nightingale to sing a song,
Beating within the heart to allow time
To be a beginning that is remade over again.
In the clothes worn by souls transforming,
A glade in the forest to be a place to share.

Red wine that smiles on the lips of hope,
Bathed in the rushing wild streams.
Quenching the thirst of rainbows coming to earth,
To stand as an oak for a millennium.
In the warm glow reflected in the tears,
Of a man that sees a ripple in focus.

-19-
PENNINE CONTACT

A black pool of ink your ship stealing all light,
Diamond with three hot stars that awoke me
On a lonely summer morning path.
Like a dark bird you hovered as I climbed,
To my feet bare on mountain grass.

ARC OF THE ANCIENTS

I stared in wonder as you opened your belly,
Beckoning me a hand with no fear
Stepping forward to climb inside of the unknown.
Wanting to see if I would be just a shiver,
In a whirlwind of fears or deliver.

Hesitating but some how sure I knew,
I walked inside to see you there ready
With a suit of blue grey you gave me the guide.
To allow shell white lines to find their place,
In hand foot head and side to be steady.

I would forever be a ship in heart,
Even as Earth shrank to a dot.
Joined together to know that,
It was the difference that saved us both
Neither slave master or toast.

I would never have believed if someone said,
That a ship needed a man to feel his way
To cure a crystal heart so they could return to the stars.
In certain knowledge that we have gifts of our own,
Without fear or favour of beings in masks.

-20-
SLEEPING AMONG THE STARS

Curled around the warmth of a star that dries your tears,
No longer running away from demons with familiar faces.
Hearing the songs that keep you safe in the echo of a heart,
That wanders the universe seeking the lonely cries
Of those who only want to be rocked to sleep.

There is no place for fear when you feel the touch,
Of stardust as you relax being kissed by the kindness
Of a universe that has many eyes to see.
If only in a dream away from the darkness,
Of those painful lonely forlorn days.

Even if you feel lost as one note in the harmony of a cosmic song,
Remember that you can feel the heart that cares.
When you listen touch the vibration that is mirrored,
In the innocent smile that a child freely gives.
Showing you the face that you know deep down,
In that secret place where monsters never reached.

When those that feed on the fear of angel's children,
Trying to strum the song of decay squeezing your tender heart.
Remember that you are the child that burns with the power of a star,
With the knowledge that the tone that makes you bright
Is part of many who like gentle shadows stand to your left and right.

They will dance in moonbeams to make you smile,
Tickle the universe to light the heavens when you are down.
Make rabbit patterns on the face of the sun,
Bring a warm glow to an ocean when they see you grin.
Sending you a rainbow that will turn any more tears,
Into peals of laughter as you see what is written in the stars.

-21-
BEYOND HEAVEN

I saw the dance of angels in a blinding light,
My wonder as I opened my heart and remembered.
What can be when we grasp that this a moment,
To be sure that a witness has been born
In a heart that will seek the truth greater than heaven's flame.

The tears fall in a winters shadow of crystal blue,
A breath disturbing the air lay the innocent asleep in the dew
In a pattern of magic that is brighter than a galaxy of stars.
Pearls of the divine manifest into grains for tiny fingers to play,
Into a harmony that will sing a new tapestry for a new day.

ARC OF THE ANCIENTS

Thus a laughing face is a dream to shatter the nightmare,
Of those can not bear joy of the timeless innocent heart,
Which is the love of the faithful to seek the untamed.
To stretch beyond the experience of the divine,
Calling all to be brave and believe in the magic of the sublime.

To seek is to find the place of a lie that demands to be told,
Shattering the bedrock of the divine is the slipstream of the watcher
Who calls those that will know that reality is but a metaphor.
To play the chord that will join the song of the deaf and blind,
So those that walk in shadows can go beyond heaven's time.

FINAL REFLECTION POEMS

-1-
NO CUDDLY LOVELY BEAR

No soft fur to lie against my cheek,
Only tears upon my face.
In the dark alone with the fear,
Of demons that clamber over me
Whose sounds haunt and torment my sleep.

Sweat trickles over goose pimpled flesh,
Nothing to clasp tight just a hard lumpy pillow.
Under a faded blanket of washed out colour,
With eyes so wide you would think they were mirrors.
Listening for those that were waiting,
For one who had a body that betrayed
The command of those that new better.

In a sea of green light that cackles and calls,
They return to dance their frightful jig.
Upon the beams that spiders do crawl,
Screaming as they mutate their bodies into hideous shapes
Until the dawn breaks upon the sound of a crashing door.

Dragged from my bed by beet red faces,
Bellowing that I once more have failed to be.
Anything other then a miserable excuse for a human being,
That doesn't deserve the comfort of a kind face.
In a soft white bear that would hold me close,
For one who is forever in heavens nocturnal disgrace.

In the attic is a corner I must stay,
To be a shadow all curled tight.
Clutching empty air to my aching chest,
Trembling in wet soiled bedtime clothes.
As I hide with a simple thought.....
"There are no cuddly lovely bears.."

-2-
SHY SPIRIT

The lights are shining and the demon is on his throne,
So you hide in the sparkle so afraid - so alone.
No one remembers your name because a fairy story,
Can never be real but to you and me.

The snow is falling and they are murdering trees,
In cities that are dying because the people refused to see.
I walk in the grey time between dreams drawn to the sigh,
As you melt into the shadow cast by a demon on his throne.

I know why you called one last time to see the colour of my tears,
To go beyond the pain of grief we shared when they shot all the deers.
The snow is stained red but your fingers guide my hand to the book,
Far below the gaze of a bored demon on his throne.

The sky fell with the comets that came to say goodbye,
When the last human could only stand and wonder why.
A candle spiked on a toe bone is all the light we need,
To paint the picture while a demon laughs on his throne.

You showed me that magic is intrinsic to all,
That a child's colouring book is misunderstood only by fools.
I will always remember your look as we showed,
That Man is the only demon now dying on his throne.

-3-
ON THE EDGE OF HEAVEN

It's all so clear this horizon that I stand upon,
To my right is the land that I know to my left a sun shining.
Inviting me to let go of the burdens and dive into a welcoming sea,
To say goodbye and be free of the demands that are stone.

The cries hurt my soul for the commitments I made,
Can I say goodbye to the land I leant could bear special fruit?
Breaking hearts that never wanted to be broken,
As fragile as my heart that slows to a whisper bidding you farewell.

One thing I know is that the dead have no voice,
Only the interpretation of those that witnessed the life.
Can I step through and be happy knowing,
That not all can be said and that words can never be enough.

Why do I hesitate to make that final step?
To watch the world fall away in the faces that I love.
The time had been placed in my hand if I design my own end,
Is the paradox leaving me stranded on an isle of mine own.

For the voices say why didn't I say the words?
When all I have ever felt is abandoned to the tide of life.
Only the hands to reach out will never reach in time,
For they can never know how naked I feel.

The saddest truth is that I don't feel worthy,
That I failed to do all that I could.
In the end I have to accept that for all time,
I could well be cursed to stand on the edge of heaven.

-4-
"WHEN THEY ASK..."

When they ask what I liked best,
I will say it was you.
A memory perfect in every way,
Is the reflection you gave that said I was ok.

It's not just about being a father,
But being able to share the boy that never knew.
To know that being a table or a chair,
Or a creature from another world was ok to share.

ARC OF THE ANCIENTS

Know my daughter that I will be here,
In whatever form you care to envision.
Like the same heart that knows the power of flight,
In the laughter of the sun's rays we have this delight.

When the time comes for tears remember,
That in each drop is your daddy's funny face.
That daft smile and mad crazy laugh,
Was only born because you understand about giraffes.

If you ever get lonely at least in one eye,
You'll see me wink with a twinkle and a smile.
Your life is an adventure that is open and full,
Cherish all the love that is open and true.

This poem like me may not have perfect rhythm,
But then what do you expect big fluffy kittens?
It may not always rhyme with time or lime,
But this is your daddy you know that chimes.

All you need to know is that I love you,
No matter where I end up because of a crazy heart beat.
You'll see me in all the pictures inside your head,
Whispering in your ear about the monkeys under the bed!

-5-
CHERISH THE FACES

Cherish the faces that say hi in the morning,
The birds that sing that lullaby and the flowers that are smiling.
No matter when the sun doesn't always shine,
Cherish the clouds that will bring the rain to kiss your blues away.

Cherish the wrinkles on the face of those that also played,
In the spring to the magical sparkle of wintertime.
In your heart is a guide that will tremble when you hear their name,
Cherish the moment when your knees give way.

Cherish the innocent face all purple and blue,
The child burping milk all over you.
No matter that you just dressed for that all important date,
Cherish the cries that say they want your face.

Cherish those faces that are dying for your time,
In the battles not always known but give you freedom all the same.
In your heart is the perfect beat when you know how to,
Cherish the steps that take you to the doorway of your destiny.

Cherish the unknown faces that connect to you,
The warmth that is shown in an act of random kindness.
No matter that they cannot see the tears or the smiles on your face,
Cherish the humanity that made sure on that day you wouldn't be late.

Cherish the world for it's more than a home but an idea,
In a moment of breathless grace.
In your heart you are vulnerable to tempestuous storms,
Cherish the lightening for it can illuminate the face before you.

Cherish the faces of your memories even the grey,
In the days that have grown you into today.
No matter that they didn't care to see the damage or their disgrace,
Cherish the fact you chose never to grow such a face.

Cherish the face that will never know your morning,
The souls that would give anything to dance in your shoes.
No matter that you can never know all their names,
Cherish the chance to go for all your aims.

Cherish the love for the face you see,
In the mirror or the one you have chosen.
In your heart is the passion to share more than you know,
Cherish all that can be for soon enough the bell will toll.

AND NOW FOR SOMETHING COMPLETELY NOT A POEM...

JUST A DREAM?

It was very odd; I was walking along a stone path. I didn't know where I was and the sky was silver. There were clouds that sparkled with tiny lights of many colours. I noticed I seemed to be closer to the path then I would normally be. Like I had shrunk I was wearing light blue pyjamas, with yellow edges to the cuffs, and to the top left pocket. I felt strange I think I remember them. A long time ago. I don't wear pyjamas, haven't done since I left home. Couldn't wear them, to many memories.

That's when he appeared. He was just there walking along side me. I know he wasn't there when I began.

"*Are you sure?*"

"Yes." I was certain. He was tall; I had to look up to see his face. Which was odd. It changed, shimmering, like he wasn't certain who he was.

"*I know, its you who are not certain.*"

"I am?"

He smiled, then wasn't. He shimmered like he was a fragmented pixel creation of a computer. Now that is odd.

"*Is everything odd to you?*"

I didn't say that, but I thought it. It wasn't strange that he understood. Now that was clear for some reason. He had long blonde hair, with dark brown eyes, and then he didn't.

Was short, slim and dark haired, then with green eyes? Then he was bald and tall, and then with blue eyes. Nose went from short to long, mouth wide to small. He had a beard then he didn't. Then he had white hair that was curly. What was the same was a suggestion of wings? But I couldn't be certain they were wings just certain that something like wings. He just shimmered too much.

But there was something old and kind, and he had a wistful, patient smile.

"*You are odd.*"

"*Yes*"

"*Why are you odd?*"

"*Do you really want to know Martin?*"

For some reason I felt shocked. How did he know my name? I didn't tell him. Did I? His features flowed again and it was hurting my eyes.

"How do you know my name?" See I did ask.

"*Because I always have.*"

I didn't understand. Just felt strange.

"*Not odd?*"

"I thought I wouldn't say that again."

"*Wise.*"

I didn't know what to say back. I just felt more confused. I looked away. I couldn't look at him any more. I didn't want to know why he was odd, so I looked at the path. I noticed my feet were bare and the path was white on grey grass. With flowers that had smiling faces made from opals. There was a sound like whales singing with a chorus of children. Then a melody of rain, and the beat of a heart. In the distance there was a mirror.

He was still there; he surprised me by taking my hand. Like I was a child. I didn't understand. His hand was warm, and I could smell flowers, and I could feel tears stinging my eyes.

"*Why do you want to cry?*"

I couldn't say anything. I was afraid. I didn't know where I was. I just felt lost. But I tried not to cry. But they leaked, and they flowed down my cheeks and I tasted salt on my lips. Then I asked.

"Who are you?"

He didn't answer and I thought he wasn't going to but when I looked up to see, the face seemed calmer, now like smooth waves that made him fluctuate but his features still changed. Maybe a bit slower.

"*I am who I am*"

That didn't help! I had a headache. I didn't understand why I was crying. My hand felt warm and slightly sweaty and I wondered if he would mind.

"*No.*"

There was no sound from my footsteps, and it was like floating a step at a time. I looked and the mirror on the road was closer. I was no longer crying. I was too surprised. I could only open my mouth and say nothing. I couldn't understand why I saw what I saw. The mirror was just there in front and we had stopped and I just stared. The surface was liquid and rippled. The image was clear. I faced an image I hadn't seen for years. This didn't make sense. I was eight again.

No glasses, no beard, short hair, sticking up, brown eyes wide between a bent nose that had only already been broken too many times. I had such small lips. The purple mark on my forehead was back. It didn't seem like me though. It was too strange. I was a grown up now. Wasn't I?

"*No.*"

I just felt dizzy and he had said no? I didn't understand. I remember growing up, going to work, not going to work. Having a daughter. Writing a book, and poems and other things. I know I did, didn't I? I kept looking in the mirror. He was there too. He looked more familiar, and he didn't flow so much. He smiled such a kind smile that I had to swallow a lump in my throat before I could say anymore.

"What do you mean – No?"

He let go of my hand and stood behind me. I looked so small, he placed large but delicate hands on my shoulders and lent down and whispered,

ARC OF THE ANCIENTS

"What do you see Martin?"

It was like a chill ran through me when he said my name again. It was so clear, like nothing I had ever heard. He said my name like it meant something, pronounced it like a crisp white sheet. I had never heard it said like that, people only ever said it like, murtan, muntin, martun, and everything in between but never like M A R T I N. Each letter a life all its own, that almost sang as they came together. I really wanted him to say it again so I could hear my name. I wasn't paying attention.

"What do you see?" He was insistent but patient and I focused on the image in the mirror and said,

"A boy." I paused and added, "A sad boy."

"Why are you sad?"

My head hurt, and my heart ached, and I didn't know what to say. I just stood blinking at the reflection. Who blinked back with tears welling up again. I could see my eyes shining and blurring so I looked at my feet. I was afraid.

"I just am..." My voice broke and I felt suddenly silly and guilty and ashamed that I couldn't answer properly. Most of all I didn't want him to know why.

"But I do know Martin and its okay."

I could feel myself go red, and I stuttered like the boy in the mirror, "I dddont undddersttand!" I flushed a deeper red. The reflection looked shocked and I felt miserable.

"Do you understand why you are here?"

"Nooo"

Then he walked round took my hand and we walked into the mirror. Into darkness, so dark that is was black. I couldn't see him but I could still smell flowers, honeysuckle, roses, bluebells, and violets. I felt the warmth of his hand and I tried not to be afraid. I tried my best not too panic. My heart was just a rapid thump thump thump. Until it stopped and I felt light headed. Pain flared through me. My left arm ached, my chest froze and my fingers felt numb in his large smooth warm hand.

Something flicked in the darkness, a light and a shadow. A small figure crept along the suggestion of a landing. With a large white sheet dragging behind. Details became clearer but everything was in shadow. I watched a boy stand by a large flat top heater. The boy struggled to drag the sheet up and in his other hand a red plastic iron. I knew this! It was just strange seeing it like this. The boy didn't notice he was being watched. He carried on struggling with the heavy sheet, putting one part then another as he ran the plastic iron over it. Over and over again. Changing the sheet round, ironing a bit then another. It was heavy and wet and I could smell the familiar aroma of warm pee. The boy looked determined, everything locked into a moment. Intense and blind.

Then a cry, a thump and everything went dark.

A scream of surprise, then a series of thumps as something fell until it stopped.Then silence.

"*You remember?*"

His voice shook me, and I jumped taking a step backwards. But he stopped me and instead of waiting for my answer he moved downwards. We floated down and down until we came to the bottom of the stairs. By the light coming through a narrow window I saw a crumpled body. In pale blue pyjamas was a dark haired boy with staring eyes, staring at nothing. Quite still, quite dead...?

"*Now do you remember?*"

No No No! I didn't. It didn't make sense. How could it be me? I remember the night I tried to dry my sheet because I wet the bed. Using my younger sister's plastic iron on the landing heater. Trying so hard to get it dry. Which took too long and I remember a sound... Then waking up in the morning. That was all. I didn't die! This was crazy.

"*But you did Martin.*"

I couldn't breathe and felt dizzy and a sick feeling that made me sway. He caught me as I fell.

I woke and I was standing in a purple field and in the centre was a well. A large brick well made up of yellow and blue and red plastic bricks! It had a green plastic roof with a black rope and on the end was a yellow bucket. He was sitting on the edge, drinking from the bucket.

I knew his name. It was surprising that I didn't remember it before. I slowly walked over and said, "Your name is Michael."

He smiled, he wore a silver and grey suit. His cream white graceful wings fluttered as he once again lifted the bucket and drank. He had dark black hair with a streak of white. A beard of grey and dark blue eyes, that was almost black. Nothing flowed; he was stable and clearer than any image I had ever seen. He glowed with an inner light and still smelt of flowers.

"*Sit.*"

We were sitting on a bench, over looking a sea, and on each wave a galaxy was born to crash into foam on a beach made from countless different shaped marbles. Like the ones I remembered. So many colours! It was so beautiful...

"*Martin...*"

"Yes," Never taking my eyes from the sea, it was mesmerising.

"*Do you know why you don't remember?*"

I kept my eyes locked on the breaking galaxies, distant to his voice but I answered.

"*No.*"

"*You were so young, you didn't want to die so you dreamed a special dream.*"

I heard him, rolling his words over my tongue, swilling it around my mind. Over and over again. Trying to make sense of something I knew was wrong. I remembered my life, it had been hard, but it had got much better. What he said couldn't be.

"This is a dream, I was sad last night and I fell asleep."

"*No. Last night you woke up.*"

I noticed my feet didn't touch the ground, I swung my legs back and forth, a breeze rippled across my pale blue pyjamas bottoms, and I tried to ignore a warning bell that sounded. A crystal tinkle that repeated over and over again. Strange I wanted to pee. But I didn't say anything trying not to listen as his firm but insistent voice rose as spoke again.

"*Have you ever wondered why in the dream you call life that you haven't died yet?*"

Now that just sounded silly. But for some reason I listened, and I saw that he may have a point.

"*From the age of eight you have been in four car crashes, you have been beaten on countless occasions, fallen off a roof, poisoned half a dozen times. Taken nine over doses, cut your wrists, ran over by a car and a lorry, drowned three times, thrown down the stairs again, and again, thrown through a window. Electrocuted eight times. Had seven heart attacks and you would say what to that?*"

I had listened to his catalogue and could have added a few more, crashed a motorbike, fallen off a mountainside, and attacked by those idiots with a knife. I was just lucky. Not that I was dead and that my life since aged eight was just a dream. That was absurd, wasn't it? But I did feel cold, and I looked up and almost lost myself in his now black eyes. I blinked and he smiled a smile that was full of sympathy and warmth.

"*You are special.*"

I didn't know what to say to that. His change of subject confused me. I just blinked at him and kept my mouth shut.

"*Don't you want to know why?*" He cupped my face in his hands, a scent of flowers was almost overwhelming and I felt dizzy again. He dropped his hands and turned towards the sea.

"*You have been here before.*" He then pointed to the ocean and on a wave a sparkle appeared. It grew as it was thrown into the air. Spinning, sending light in all directions until it landed in his hand. It was a clear crystal, with what looked like a spiral galaxy inside. He shook the crystal like it was one of those snow domes and slowly a picture appeared.

It was a scene of woodland at night, and a man was crouched by a lakeshore. He was putting shells into his dressing gown pocket. He looked up and flew into the air, hovered for a moment then sped down the track into the woods. The man smiled as he flew over the heads of some people. He knew he couldn't be seen. He was having a good dream. He then used a light to see where he was going and became amused when he found that if he shone the light into peoples faces, they blinked and looked round totally confused. He did it a few times, looked a little shame faced and stopped. Turned and twisted in mid air and made his way to the place that the people seemed to be heading for. Over their heads and into a large barn. It was full of people, sitting round, drinking and talking. The man floated down and sat at a table. It was almost full, and they were busy talking. He knew they couldn't see him. Helped himself to a drink, a cigarette and just watched. Then suddenly someone spoke and the Man looked startled. He had been seen. But the person who spoke was kind and told him he couldn't stay. He had to go now but before he could the person showed him a newspaper headline. I couldn't make it out but it was something important. Then I looked closer at the Man and the person and realised it was Michael and myself.

So we had met before, and if my life was a dream, and this scene was a dream within a dream, what does it mean?

"*Martin...*" He almost seemed to hesitate, but it could have been a pause for breath, "*You remember what happened next?*"

"Yes." I did, I had left by shifting, flowing out of the picture, into another, and another. I remembered at one point waking up in a strange bed, looking at the sleeping face of beautiful women who I knew I dearly loved, then feeling the loss, as I faded out to another place that was fear. A place that manifested fear as a force to be faced. I had done so, taking all I had learned and without killing the manifestation; it had been weird, a creature half machine half monster and with flails for arms that tried to rip me apart. All I did was be quick enough to catch the ends and tie the creature up. Then I had floated and was shifted to a point where I woke up.

Michael, his head to one side as if listening to my thoughts, which he most likely was from what I knew so far, just stared at me.

"*Now this is how it really was. You woke up on the lakeshore, you came to this world, the place you walk, when you do not dream of the life that was stolen from you. I told you to go back, as you were not ready to wake up and stay in this world.*"

As I was listening to him speak, only the second time he had spoken so fully, I realised how normal I felt. I felt like I was my normal 37 not 8! I looked down and I was wearing that same dressing gown. The one I wear when I sit at night in my room writing.

Michael just shook his head and sighed.

"*Martin you are special my friend because you are one of the few who suspect the truth. In the dreams of your dream why do you so often dream of your own death? Why do you not bruise...?*"

What he said was true, I do often dream of my death, in different times, past, present and future and its also true I don't bruise. Haven't done since I was...

I felt so chilled and I really didn't want to go. I felt so alone. I saw it all fade. His final words will stay.

ARC OF THE ANCIENTS

"It won't be long now, and soon you will be able to let go of your dream and for the last time wake up here to stay."

I woke up.

But I wonder was that just a dream or is this? And what of the rest of you?

THE END...

AND FINALLY...

THE SPIRIT OF CHISHARNLAY

In the cosmos of spirit there is no time, many have said this..........
So here is a concept for you.... I call it *Chisharnlay*..... When everyone dies we all meet in one glorious wave, an explosion of particles of light and love that embraces all. This wave breaks upon all the shores of time, carrying all to meet, one moment, one single expression of the time that was, that is and will be. The final chorus of a life form that will turn and break new ground upon many shores, sending ever increasing circles that ripple across the face of reality, making new times, new lives that will define new horizons that make the colours of rainbows for all to see. Your wave will appear to intersect time, dropping you off on the way, born on this day, and dying on the morrow you may return to yesterday, to be a child in a land of yesteryear, There is no restriction no time that bars your way, a choice to be in a moment of temporal history that you choose.

With no linear path, just a warm wave that bring you to your shore... By letting go of time's illusion that says today is today and tomorrow is tomorrow and yesterday is yesterday... The freedom is yours to find your own way... To be the ending and the beginning and the now is cherished moment.... that is the song of Chisharnlay...

A PREVIEW – THREE PARTS OF THE BLOODFIRE SAGA ©Copyright 2001

THE CLAN OF THE BLOODFIRE
1.

Atorn grunted, heaving on the coarse fibre rope, sending the next pallet of pale yellow stone up to the waiting stonemasons. The wooden block creaked in protest as the load ascended and with one final pull, the pallet reached the eager hands of the men hollering at him to get the next load ready. He cursed them as he cursed the building of the tower, the centrepiece for his master's palace. His shaggy fur was not helping matters, he was used to the cold heights of the mountains and not this lowland dust bowl. He stretched and yawned, his greats arms reaching up, knocking the fast descending pallet now empty of its load. It bounced off him, hitting the lower wall then swung back, the rope screaming in protest. The simple wooden base shuddered once, gave up the idea of being useful and disintegrated. Showing his agility Atorn skipped backwards, managing to miss the head of the man who was bending over the lime mixing trough but did not miss the trough itself. His left foot, all hair and claws sank into the burning mix. It didn't register at first as he was too busy avoiding the falling timbers but when it did, he looked back, frowned in annoyance and shook his foot free. Unfortunately it sent burning lime over the artisan who screamed clawing at his now burning head.

Atorn swore, grabbed the man by the hair and threw him in the direction of the water barrel in the yard. Not checking to see if his aim was true, he looked down at the gooey mess of his right foot. Faint curls of smoke wafted up, the hairs happily burning away. It wasn't his day.

"Hey the poor sod is drowning!"

A sound of running feet and Atorn looked up in time to see the artisan being hauled out of the barrel. Going by how much his legs were kicking Atorn took it as a good sign that the artisan was still alive. Deciding he had seen quite enough he turned and stomped out of the yard, through the south gate to the rows of red tiled buildings that served as quarters for the workers. He chose to ignore the choice words that were thrown his way as the men glared at him as he passed.

Atorn's mood didn't improve as he bent double to get inside the doorway. Taking a hand full of straw, enough to make a normal mans bedding; he walked over the patterned tile floor to the open bathhouse beyond. Big enough for twenty people, it was only just big enough for his great bulk to sink into. It was just deep enough for the hot steaming waters to reach his waist. Muttering under his breath he used the now damp straw to clean his foot. The lime cement had already started to harden, but with a few rough strokes he managed to nock most of it free. It didn't take long, but his foot did look rather odd. Pink and red with no fur at all, his claws polished white by the reaction of the lime and water. He rested his foot on the blue ceramic side of the communal bath and stared at it. Then stretched his left leg and rested that beside it and compared the two. He was not happy; he was going to look really strange now.

He was considering whether he should go and sink his other foot into the lime cement to get a matching pair when through the blanket of steam he caught sight of a figure coming closer. He didn't need to see who it was, the soft chuckling made it apparent that his lord and bloomin master had come to gloat!

"Now would I do that?"

"You already are!" growled Atorn, trying his best to glare at him but the steam made that a bit pointless. The steam wrapped figure attempted to lower itself into the pool, tried to shove Atorn's leg out of the way, but it was rather like trying to move a giant tree trunk. Grumbling Atorn moved his leg allowing his master to descend.

"Umm in spite of the terrible smell that you are stinking the place up with, this isn't half bad."

Ignoring the insult Atorn wafted away enough of the steam to see Kyedane more clearly, so he could glare at him more effectively.

"Oh that's nice, lovely draft, you wouldn't mind doing that some more?"

Atorn gave a warning growl, "I am not in the mood for your infantile humour!"

"Oh you are in a bad mood aren't you?" Kyedane's pale golden eyes sparkled with mischief adding, " Well you have wrecked the rest of the days work, the men won't work with you anymore."

"They wont work with me!" Roared Atorn, bringing his fist up and shook it in Kyedane's face. "Those ungrateful little bastards!"

Laughing Kyedane tried wiping the water from his face. Atorn's hairy fist, soaked with water was showering over him.

Between gasps for breath, and gulping the odd drop of water he managed to choke out, "Okay... okay, enough Atorn!"

Realizing that he was half drowning his lord and master Atorn lowered his fist and scratched his hairy matted chest.

Wiping the water from his eyes, Kyedane chuckled, "Well I did come in here for a bath, the shower was an extra bonus!" and grinned up at Atorn's scowling face.

He tried to keep the scowl in place, but the idiotic grin of Kyedane's made it difficult and he turned away in case a smile escaped. The tension of the day was fast being soaked away and realizing he couldn't stay angry with his master for long, he gave in and allowed a rumble of mirth to chuckle deep inside.

Kyedane being used to Atorn's mood noticed the subtle quiver of repressed mirth but decided not to comment on it in case it spoilt the mood. He instead continued to tread water and slowly moved over to Atorn's left leg, grabbing a handful of hair, he hauled himself up, so he could sit on the mass of muscle and hair.

Atorn watched his master getting himself comfortable on his leg, caught by the simple fact of how small these creatures were. They were so unlike his people. Puny in size but capable of actions that were giant in scope and thought. Maybe that was why he was reasonably fond of them, and being Guardian to this one wasn't so bad. But it did grate that he was being used as workhorse. It was not very dignified!

Brushing back his dark wet hair, and relieving his silver streaked beard of the water that was causing it to itch Kyedane picked up Atorn's mood and gently said, "I know you are not happy, and as things stand, the men can finish the tower."

"Good!"

"Right now that's settled," grinned Kyedane, "I have something to show you, so finish your bath and I'll meet you in the valley of Hyeramin at dusk." Not waiting for an answer he slid of Atorn's leg and swam to the side and pulled himself out of the bath.

"Ahh! Kyedane!"

"Yes Atorn?"

"I think you better go and take another bath!" His laughter exploded out of him, and the room shook. Kyedane put his hands up to cover his ears, which didn't help, it just made Atorn roar even louder with laughter.

Kyedane shook his head and strode out of the bathhouse.

It was only when the women of the cold room, who lowered their eyes, and turned their faces to hide their smirks and gently turned him to the bronze mirror that he saw why. He was hairier than Atorn! From head to toe he was covered in Atorn's red brown fur and his ears had tufts of hair growing out of them where he had held up his hands to stop his ear drums being burst by Atorn's laughter.

"The Bastard...He's moulting!"

The ladies of the bathhouse collapsed in hysterics...

* * *

THE KEEP OF THE BLOODFIRE
2.

The Keep stood at the centre, three times the height of the twelve Blue stones, each over ten cubits high. The crowd was in chaos, running to and fro among the stones, each one daring the other to throw spears in an attempt to find a target through the vertical slits that were all the Keep had for windows. Most just clanged against the marble streaked stonewalls, falling back on those that were too close. The Clan were impotent in their anger. The edifice that they broke themselves on would never be breached. They had no siege equipment. No real organisation and the attempt to light fires around the Keep had failed to do anything but smear the marble with black smoke stains. Among the cries, and screams of anger were the laughter of children who joined their parents in the attack no better than a rain drop on a mountain. They would never wear it down and soon harsh words were exchanged as the Clan began to break up.

Atorn watched the rabble as it began to disintegrate. In small groups they slowly drifted away, many with red faces, covered in grime and sweat. Their animal hide cloaks hanging haphazardly from unhinged clasps. His smile was grim with wry amusement at the futile attempt by the Clan.

The sky, deep orange with oppressive black clouds, seemed to hang lower. A light patter of rain fell, then cracks of lightning that streaked down to light the valley in blue flashes. The people below his hill top vantage point shrank inside their cloaks, some having to use their round wooden shields to save themselves from the downpour. A group of women in rich blue stained cloaks, with the golden Torcs that marked them as the Clan's spiritual Warriors, stood silent at the entrance to the Stone circle. With cool black eyes they appraised the Keep. Twelve who had watched with their own silent thoughts, at the stupidity of the men who had demanded the attempt in the first place.

It had been argued that man could not kill a Dark God but then the voice of the Priestess has stated that it would be women who would succeed where man failed. It had taken them time to delve into all the law that, within the traditions of the Clans, passed to each Priestess who was the voice of the Earth Goddess. The ritual of the Earth Fire would be directed by blood. No one had argued against this, however no one but the Spiritual Warriors would take a hand. The law of the Clan had demanded one more try, so this day had been marked and the pledge to mankind kept.

ARC OF THE ANCIENTS

The building of the Keep was a mystery; it had appeared in the centre of the stone circle during a harsh winter that had kept the Clans away from the upper valley. Confined to the lower there were no witnesses to its construction. They didn't know how something so large could be built to stand above ground. They had their own stone keeps, a few cubits high, wrought from raw stone. They could shift the giant moniliths to create their stone circles but they had yet to learn the art of construction to these heights. All they knew that when it drew dark, death came in the shape of a man who turned blood to fire and consumed those that didn't hide deep in the bowls of their underground cairn. Only the words of magic spoken by the Priestess saved them at night, in that place of ceremony and worship. But water had to be fetched, a child brought in, or animals protected against other beasts. There was a limit to how many could be squeezed in and the brave few who chose to stay atop paid the price.

The memory of those that had screamed in fear during the night, to a morning when only ash remained to show that once a soul had laughed and played upon the earth, burned bright as Ch'an watched dusk descend.

A few of the younger children strayed on the edge, laughing throwing stones and running away then turning, some using sling shots made from wild boar hide, managed to get a few through the dark slits. With more and more of the clan drifting away, the children were grabbed by the scruff of the neck and dragged away, protesting loudly that it just wasn't fair.

A young boy, no more then six cycles of the sun, ran giggling into the group of women. With out hesitation an iron knife flashed and the boy dropped. His throat slit. Those that saw turned their faces and hurried on. None had courage to face the obsidian eyes that glared at them as they passed. No man could face their shame at the price they had agreed would be met to save themselves reflected in those dark eyes that accused them as they passed. The rain bent them double, hiding them further as the women picked up the body and laid it on the mica grey stone behind them. The blood mixed with the rain ran quickly down the groove to be collected in a large copper bowl at the foot of the stone.

The urge to run down the hill, to coalesce into a form that would have made even these frighteningly determined women scream in panic, was hard to resist. Atorn swallowed down his anger remaining as a faint haze of mist clinging to the wild flowers that covered the hill. He had to wait; the sun was just beginning to set. The last few of the clan were now far along the dirt track that wound along the valley floor, most of it running parallel to a fast flowing river that frothed and tumbled, laping at the reed filled bank.

The fires had long gone out and as the gloom broadened, a few wisps of smoke were fast fading and the women lit the grease bowls. Each had a cover made from treated birch bark, allowing them to be used in the rain. Each one placed around the entrance altar stone. The cowls of their cloaks were now up, saving them from the worse of the rain. The animal grease lanterns could be smelt on the wind that gusted in swirls around the stones. None of them paid attention to the strange mist that slowly edged towards them.

The landscape once green and lush under the sun was now a brooding place of mean yellow light that was too selfish to break more than hand's width of darkness. The crystal in the Blue stones began to glow, adding an extra dimension to the scene. The swirls of blue on the tan hides of the cloaks were shimmering, making the fat that waterproofed them glisten with rain and reflected light. The women poured scented oil over the boy; his slim form, naked now upon the stone, was an insult to Atorn's sense of what he considered to be right. While the twelve women continued their preparations he snuck a little closer.

The Priestess glanced up catching the movement but didn't respond even though it was odd to see a ground mist with so much rain. The thunder continued to bear down, and streaks of lighting forked down to lance themselves against the Keep, which was now just a black shadow in the centre. No movemement came from there and the women paid no heed as gem-studded knives began to appear in each red swollen hand. A low hum of murmering voices rose up, increasing in volume and cadence changing as archaic words began to be woven into a cloth that wrapped the boy like a shroud of intent.

With a cry that was powerful enough to silence thunder, twelve knives slashed down. The body long since drained of its meagre supply of blood was quickly and mercilessly dispatched into slabs of meat ready for the next phase of the ritual.

Ch'an broke from the rest and carrying the bloody heart turned away and walked to the base of the Keep. The litanies of words were now just a whisper as she knelt and placed the heart at the foot of the wrought iron door.

Atorn was among them, swirling around, dancing among the lights, ignored by all as the rest of the women took their handful of flesh and placed each piece round the Keep. Atorn looked at the mess they had made of the boy. There was not much left. The chest cavity, open to the rain, was being washed clean. The boy's face was just a frozen mask of surprise, eyes that only a short time ago were sparkling with laughter cried with tears of rain. He did feel pity and a wave of sadness washed over him as he began to coalesce.

First only a shadow formed, seemingly covering the remains of the boy hiding him from a now silent sky. The rain reduced to a drizzle, faded away and the clouds broke up to allow a velvet black sky appear. One by one stars twinkled into life forming constellations and a broad swath of stars that snaked its way across the sky. Using his senses he reached out and drew what was left of the boy into himself. The body flared with light then was gone.

Atorn turned round, gave a back kick shattering the blood stained stone. Shards flew in all directions, passing harmlessly through him. Then he gave a twist and grabbed them so they hung in mid flight waiting for his command.

The twelve Spiritual Warriors were deep in their induced trance, all thought bonded as one and each heart as one beat. No care for anything but the task in hand. The power they drew on flowed from the Blue stones that drank deep from the energy of the earth. None were aware of the creature that stood watching them. Atorn stood higher than the Stones, his red brown shaggy haired body, lit only by the raising light that throbbed in time with the Priestess's own heartbeats, braced between the two entrance stones. His hands, larger than the flattened tops, dug deep like a hot knife into flesh, his yellow ivory claws joined with stone. Blue light flashed through him as he redirected the energy that the women were using. The shards of broken stone quivered, their place at heart level seemed to strain to be free as they faded from view, warped out of faze by Atorn's will.

Deep within the trance the voice of the twelve women formed one note that broke free, lancing energy into the flesh, consuming it to ash, which soaked into the grass like grey wine.

A tremor shook the ground and the Keep wavered, the marble facing cracked, falling pieces passing within finger length of the women who were still bowed directing the spell that would destroy the place that hid a creature which had with impunity ravaged the surrounding clans for six seasons.

Now it was Ch'an's task as leader to finish it. She placed her hand on the heart, that no tear of sentiment could bring back, and spoke the final word.

The Keep buckled but still standing, shimmered once then vanished.

She looked up surprised and turned to the others in shock. It was only then when the two women on either side barked out an order that Ch'an turned to see the thing that towered above them. Standing, still connected to the stones, was a giant covered in fur, with teeth that were hooked over black lips. It glowed with blue fire, and it wasn't looking at them.

It roared once and the two blue entrance stones shattered but collapsed into fist sized fragments and fell into piles at the creature's yellow stained feet.

As one, the women stood up and with one mind roared their reply for the desecration of their holiest of sites. The keep was gone, how they had managed that when the intent had been to reduce it to rubble the same way that... All that energy redirected, Ch'an now knew they had been cheated and their wrath was immense.

Atorn dizzy from his labour to save the home of his master Kyedane didn't see the energy bolt that blasted into him. He was flung back, falling into the space that the altar stone had left. The ground shook as he landed. Fully formed he was like an enormous oak falling.

The women now determined and without fear rushed towards him, gold knives poised to carve what they could from the desecrator. The earth fire was gone, the connection broken, and magic no longer an option they turned to their kill as Warriors. Trained by those of the far south -The Head Priestess of Isis had taught Ch'an in the tomb of their Gods and she knew her art well.

They were twelve ants darting this way and that over his smoking bulk. The blast had caught him in the chest and Atorn had to admire their spirit as they tried to find away to make him bleed. He lay contemplating the pattern in the stars. Taking note that he had managed to shift the Keep to a new location, and at least a thousand years into the future. But he couldn't have done it without the help of those that were now clambering on top of his hairy chest.

He almost laughed out loud when he felt a weight on his forehead but to his horror that broke when he felt pain lance into his eyes. That was the last thing he saw.

She had come up from behind him and had run and somersaulted to land neatly on his head. Another dive forward over the brow, her arms outstretched, twisting herself over to land on her snout. Her arms almost twisted out of her sockets but even her tiny weight, in comparison to his, was enough to plunge them deep.

He roared in pain and rolled over squashing four of the women.

Ch'an dived once more and managed to land on her feet. One call and the remaining women ran to her side. Cloaks had been torn off, and ash bows were unstrapped and arrows notched by the time the beast had rolled back.

It was almost beyond belief for Atorn to be caught out like that; he was angry, but some how amused. Considering what the clan had suffered there had to be a price. Rather him than Kyedane! But sometimes his job as Guardian had annoying points to it! The better part of valour... He ignored the women who he could sense were about to have another go, and dissipated.

Eight arrows thudded into grass and bare earth. Ch'an glared at the mist that began to break up, drifting away until nothing remained. She turned, realising that the damage to the circle was far worse. Three of the other stones had fallen; she and the others hadn't noticed that. Two reduced to rubble, and where was the grey altar stone? And the Boy! She didn't let despair take her, she could do nothing to honour the bones of the child. All she could do was her duty.

With that in mind Ch'an and the remaining Warriors picked up their cloaks, closed the gold torcs and walked over to pick up their precious arrows. They had been a gift from Isis, a trade for gems dug from the mountains to the north.

ARC OF THE ANCIENTS

The circle had been broken, but there were plans for a greater circle further south on the great plain, by the lakes and marshes of the Wurm. The remaining Blue stones would have a new home soon enough and the Earth Magic would once more rise. She and the others would bury their dead and go home. No matter how, they had stopped the ravage of the Bloodfire, and scored one success against whatever that thing had been. For today it was over.

Atorn turned the pages of time until he came to the place that would begin the next phase. In this time a battle was about to start, the inheritors of this land, long after Ch'an and her kind were dust, were facing a new threat. Soldiers who held the standard of the Eagle and the might of a far place called Rome. The time of the Earth Goddess would be finished on this day and the age of man would truly begin. There was the matter of the stone shards still quivering to let fly. Today would be their day... Another blood sacrifice would pay for another journey for his charge, sleeping deep within the safe walls of a Keep from another age.

THE COMING OF THE BLOODFIRE
3.

There is no dream, just pointless ever ending darkness and why is it so cold? That is the trouble with tombs; the cold seeps in, making the silk lining damp and musty. Now the cold just reminds me that my existence is pointless, and such a waste of dead flesh.

You once said, Can I plant a tree? It would brighten the place up.

Not unless you want to dig up ten feet of stone!

Do you remember trying to turn yourself over in one of these things? I try to turn and the bottom padding slips, the bottom sheet then slides up, and I try to pull it down and before I know I've twisted over, half wrapped, and partly spun like wool on a spindle.

Like the colour though, interesting shade of purple. See now I'm really bound up!

Breathe breathe! Did you know that it tightens as you struggle? I'm relaxing, trying my best not to panic. Last thing I need is to get claustophic in here.

My mind keeps trying to hold on to a memory.

Ok I'm calmer now. Why can't I see? Why does your face fade? I find no comfort in this empty dreamless sleep. It's too much I know, to torture myself with your memory that doesn't have the courtesy to stay.

Why does my mind keep turning all I say into some strange poetic nonsense?

I might get complaints.

I know it is coming; I wouldn't be here trying to figure out why I am here, waking up with the feeling that my brain has decomposed on me.

You know I do want to return to the sky and begin my search for you.

How many times can I do this? When will I find peace? When will you return to grace the world above this place?

At least I won't need a shave, as my beard doesn't grow when I sleep. Its still the silver with black streaks that you loved to stroke.

Remember you used to trim it for me?

I can hear a faint buzzing, I hope its not wasps again, or those really horrible blue flies!

If I'm not careful I'll be screaming like a banshee in a minute.

Ok calming myself.

It's just the shallow minds of those that are more sand then true flesh. Now that made no sense! This is so uncomfortable when I wake up. See, the silken pillows move and I'm facing the dark stone of my lonely tomb. That's quite poetical...

ARC OF THE ANCIENTS

I can sense the sun beginning to set; I'll wait until there is no more warmth.

It only takes a good heave, and the slab is pushed aside. Gripping hard on the granite stone, levering myself up and over the side. Using the sight that needs no eyes I pick out the walls, the place, in a cave lost in the middle of a dank catacomb.

It's like thinking in the form of a badly constructed novel! What was that word! Staid! What ever does that mean? Oh grave! Now that is funny!!

Home, bitter home. Holds no warmth, no fire that awakens the flesh to the possibility of the power to cause dream to transform reality.

Do you know how cold my bottom is? Doesn't help sitting here on the edge of my tomb.

There is no use in pondering things I cannot yet change. There is only the itch that causes me to reach out and turn the darkness into the blaze of candlelight. Shifting shadows move as I walk stiffly, flexing joints that should have been dust, to the other side of the hall of our buried keep.

I hate having crusty eyes when I wake up. Even the light from candle flame hurts.

I know, I will resist the temptation to rub them. Must be some water somewhere in here...

Crunch!

Ouch that hurts! Oh its the long table where I dined alone, musing over you. You wouldn't be pleased, it's very dusty with cobwebs strangling the tarnished silver plate, cups, and knives. Your entire best cutlery. Now its just reminders of memories of better times, and your chairs of ebony wood lay broken, scattered like limbs torn from a tired tree.

I think my mind is broken, something is fractured, and so stiff but then you were not here, I walked around here for a hundred years before I gave up and went to sleep.

It smells bad too, damp with spores from the faint glowing clusters of fungi that are slowly reclaiming the wood panels and half empty bookshelves that line the north and south walls.

You would not be amused.

Sorry but I forgot to water your plants, I think they will be dead now.

How long this time? How long have I been asleep? Would it be a month or a year or a few decades? In this place where time no longer touches the grey flesh that is carrying my hungry soul to the blackened iron door, where the diamond studded handle shines mocking the decay around me.

Complete insanity, I have been asleep for too long.

I want to touch that light, to see if I can feel any warmth that my flesh is denied. Almost like I could kindle the fire by stealing a little of its own, but I don't, I just stand hesitating...

You can see why?

I wish you could answer me!

But if you did then I would be insane.

I don't think you will mind me telling you all this... I mean if I don't try, I might go a bit insane. Have I had that thought before? Only a bit.

What am I waiting for? Am I so tired and scared that I cannot dare venture beyond these crumbling old walls? With my left hand I'm brushing the dust from my faded black trousers?

The silver gold cuff links you gave me are making sparkling bouncing patterns against the wall. Pretty...

I can feel the hunger rising inside me, testing my cowardice, to see how long I can stand here procrastinating.

My right hand is going to surprise me, I know!

A touch.

Blinking in surprise that hurt! I knew I had forgotten something.

The door has vanished, and I am outside, brass holders in the walls, drinking cups for fire flies burst into flame to light the red brown clay and stone passage way.

Did I forget? There is no memory of this transition, how can that be? I am walking in a day that is filled with puzzlement.

I know something is very wrong, but I can't think why. So there is nothing left but to walk, so I walk. My blue velvet cloak, clasped round my neck by two cats chewing on each other's tail, flap against my legs as I walk on. The passage is lined with cups that are lighting my way. Each turn and twist, the lights just appear, no command from me. Like it was ready for me? This makes no sense; I remember something of the time before I had to return to my sleep.

The screams of fire, the battle that tore the heart from me, and the destruction and chaos of the war that killed so many. I remember the vacant eyes; I remember the blue light go dark, your lips bloody and torn. Your auburn hair shorn from your head by those that wore the mark of the hunters. But for all my effort I cannot conjure your complete face.

I can smell you!

"You can?"

"No not you Atorn, her! I really wish you wouldn't interrupt when I talk to her – I mean its not if I do it aloud! Its called talking to her in my mind, trying to reach her! Besides its rude to interrupt my thoughts!"

"Ok."

Silence...

Exotic, sweet, pungent crisp taste, dripping with dew, stolen from the gods who dwell beyond the Arc. Were they that jealous of our love that they had to take you from me?

Will my mind stop spewing this crap?

ARC OF THE ANCIENTS

I feel the fire spasm inside my chest, burning, urging me on. The memory is fading...

But a smile!

I see lips curved, teeth of ivory and the heat that ignites.

Smack!

Rubbing my head, I look up and realise that I just walked into an old rusty grate, with a low brick archway. No more memories, I leave those and reach out to open this, the last barrier to the world above. It creaks, squeals in protest. But slowly it's opening. The sound is echoing down the passageway, a flutter and a thousand leathery wings brush overhead.

Hope you are getting all this!

I am here, on grass, wet with a nighttime dew. The bats fly off, curving round a tree, to skim and dart around a bright yellow light. That seems to hang from a neck of iron, so big! Unless it's a tree of some unknown type? But no branches, just a stem with a neck! Unless it's a creature that my memory had lost? If so why is it so still? I can feel the breeze, smell grass, pollen and something else, something rancid, sharp, biting and it's rapidly reducing my sense of smell!

You wouldn't like it at all. Things have changed!

A park! The word distracts me as it flips into existence inside my mind.

I rub my hand across the grass; the dew is cool and most importantly wet!

You could have warned me that I was kneeling in the grass. That's better though, lovely to feel cool water in my eyes.

My legs are creaking as I stand. So where is the village?

The village that I knew is now a faded memory but it should have been here! The mud and wattle houses of the peasants, the steep terraced lines of cultivated crops. The distant wall of willow stakes guarding the perimeter. Beyond that the pasture lands of the lower valley.

I remember eating here!

Used to watch the fires being lit to guard against man or beast, and the circle of stones that marked the last raising of earth fire a generation before.

You danced for me then, I remember the blue light and your pale skin sparking with a thousand fires blossoming through your skin, making every curve, a sensuous line and, and now its all gone...

The park, a word that is seeping further into my brain is like a poison, from a well-aimed arrow. Foreign but familiar. None of this is making sense.

It's all in shadow, a grey path winds through more trees. My eyes search and I am walking and hoping for something familiar?

The fire burns brighter; I can feel it begin to pump energy back into my body.

Can you feel that?

No you are quite dead, and I am walking in a world that is just as dead to me.

This is the last reserve of energy before I fall and return to dust, broken by time.

More lights, more strange trees, then...

What! No!

Towers stretching into the sky, blazing with lights, a hundred or more squares of white and yellow. I am craning my neck, trying to see how high they go.

I wish you could see this.

Turning round and round in utter shock.

"I know you are making me dizzy!"

So I stop.

"Thank you... Kyedane."

"You have a really soft voice for a spirit, Atorn but at the moment I'm slightly distracted, my eyes are locked on the building opposite this park."

"I would rather you told me what are you looking at?"

I can't say, Atorn will have to wait for an answer, I can no longer open my mouth and all I see is...

Oh Leaynaa! - Your face is on the building! Like a frozen reflection clearer then I have ever seen. A kind of magic that I am unaware, or maybe just forgotten existed.

Your hair is different, more variation in tones, from auburn I knew, to flecks of gold and your eyes are bright, dark sapphires and you are smiling with laughter, your lips so big and bright and deep dark red...

Leaynaa...

The fire is burning like acid in my veins, opening them up to blood that is starting to pump from a heart that hasn't beaten for... Well I have yet to find out!

Holding my left hand up, I see the skin shimmer as colour floods the grey and the tell tale sign of the sunburst ignites turning into a diamond shape of gold that is becoming solid as I watch.

Crouched below my index and mid fingers a tiny stud glimmers from the light above my place on the edge of a park, across from a street that has buildings that almost touch the stars.

I can feel a hand on my shoulder; I know that it's not you – Leaynaa but Atorn that is waiting for me to speak, so I will.

"I take it Atorn that they are buildings, and before I go any further how long has it been since I took my sleep?"

"Yes, and its been four thousand, seven hundred and twenty nine years, four months, three days, ten hours, and five minutes, and twenty three seconds."

"You are always so precise." It was automatic, like I had said it a hundred times before, which obviously I had. Then the shock hit. I think its getting dark again, why is it so fuzzy all of a sudden?

ARC OF THE ANCIENTS

"Because my friend you are fainting!" Atorn couldn't help the chuckle, he may be a spirit that has walked the earth for twelve thousand years but he still found amusement in the little things in life.

Atorn waited, standing over his friend, his shaggy coat coming into focus, unlike his eyes which had been torn out, on a day too many years to count. In an age that he knew those that existed in this time, had no idea existed at all? Damn he's getting me at it now!

He looked up at the building opposite; he knew what he was looking at. He may be blind in the conventional sense but he had extra senses that made up for it. He wouldn't be much good as a Guardian if he didn't. Atorn also knew that Kyedane was too brain dead to realise that.

He had been around watching for long enough to know that the picture of Leaynaa was nothing more than an advertisement for a soft drink and a computer game, with the lady created from the imagination of a computer. Or the human that programmed it. He was not sure how it all worked but he did know that Kyedane would not be happy when he figures it out.

He also knew that Kyedane would tear this world apart to find the real Leaynaa when he did figure it out. No he wouldn't be happy if he knew that the image was nothing more than a very clever computer graphic.

If Kyedane succeeded in finding her then the world the humans knew would end in the Bloodfire, and it would be up to Atorn to prevent it.

Could he betray his friend? Protector and Traitor in one breath.

Come to think of it he could. It wasn't so bad once the decision had been made. Now all he had to do was wait for the others that could smell the latest pyre's being lit, to come and lay claim to a creature that would be herald as master and saviour of a new world.

Atorn couldn't afford to fail...

The picture winked at him, it made his fur rise in alarm, and Atorn scolded himself for being so jittery. It was only a distraction, something to keep Kyedane alive, hopeful but going utterly in the wrong direction. It would be up to Atorn to track down the real Leaynaa and kill her before Kyedane found out that Atorn his friend and mentor was an utter bastard.

The smell made him turn his head, on the hills above the city he could feel the heat, the smell of burning flesh, of the blood sacrifice that men had used to change time itself to bring the triad into beginning. How many was it up to, One million? He wondered if any of the pale humans knew that they were killing more than sheep and cows but a future?

A screech of tyres, a car stopped. They paid Atorn no attention, they were not bright enough to see him, but he could certainly smell them, see them in all the ways that mattered. They picked up Kyedane. Looking like bad extra's from a very bad movie – with complimentary dark glasses as well!

Doors slammed, and they were gone.

He had something else to do and began to lope down the street.

He might have time to catch one of those movies, but for now he had an urgent appointment for dinner.

There was nothing to see for any late night revellers, just a few scraps of paper that fluttered in the air as he ran by, with words that announced the postponement of an election.

Now that Atorn found extremely amusing.

*   *   *

The apartment was spacious, all clean lines and very little clutter. The maid had been in which was why Lou Lou could find the Census form. She had put it somewhere safe, but as everything seem to have a mind of its own it was often the case she had a hard trouble finding anything.

The evening sun shone clear and bright making the living room warm and cosy. Pots of flowers dotted the room, the only splashes of colours that broke the neat white walls. All the furniture was a sharp almost cold white. Contrasting sharply with her black leather jacket thrown over the deep cushioned chair, and the black tee shirt and black leather trousers she wore, now curled up on the long curved sofa that she melted into. Feet curled under, a cup of black coffee steaming on the glass crystal table in front of her. With one hand she picked up the remote, and flicked the button to turn on the white encased TV, and the other she opened the form.

She was bored, so the census was just to pass some time until she made up her mind what to zap for dinner. Lou Lou paused at the page that asked what religion she was, which made her chuckle as she almost wrote Jedi, but instead wrote Chisharnlay.

"Now that will give their computers something to ponder over, hope it blows a fuse!" laughing to herself. She had received an email about the idea to put Jedi on the form, which she thought was a great idea. It had been said that if 10,000 people filled in with Jedi, then it would be enough to create a new religion! Which would be a great laugh. To think of thousands of Jedi Knights going round saying, "May the force be with you!" and protected from being nutters by the law that protects all recognised religions! But then after reading a new novel called Exodus: The Dolph/in Saga, by a very gifted and obviously talented writer, the idea of using the author's name for the Dolph/in's idea of heaven seemed just that tiny bit more of a lunatic idea which appealed to her enormously.

She giggled as she admired her handy work, she had written in big letters; C H I S H A R N L A Y So the computer scanners wouldn't miss it, she was just being helpful.

ARC OF THE ANCIENTS

Looking up she saw that the news was starting, so she turned the volume up.

Oh it was John Snow! For some reason she found him very sexy, maybe it was his voice that commanded attention, or the fact that she couldn't really imagine him as an owl. She giggled at the mental picture.

He did his usual side angle to camera and pronounced, "Tonight on Channel 4 news, we ask the question; is Tony Blair still fit to be prime minister?" a pause, his eyes twinkling making Lou Lou almost purr in anticipation.

"After the recent mass culling of two million animals, the refusal to vaccinate, and the increase in toxins in the atmosphere from the burning pyre's. Combined with the events of today, which saw more protests over the cull, highlighted by the white calf saved, and I quote ' From the murdering hands of MAFF'. Causing the suspension of the cull of healthy Cattle, while the cull of all affected sheep and pigs will continue.

"We ask a leading psychologist, is Tony Blair Insane? And we give you your chance to tell us what you think.

"Phone on 0193 456 001 for Yes or 0193 456 02 for No, we will give the results at the end of the programme. Now for the rest of the headlines here is…"

She was just glad she wasn't drinking her coffee; otherwise she would have ruined her nice white sofa with spattered coffee stains. Lou Lou still wasn't convinced she heard that right! The trill of her mobile phone interrupted her train of thought. Trouble was where had she put it?

The census form fell to the floor as she leant over the sofa, looking under the coffee table, that was clear, only a faint outline of a red stain marked the pristine white high pile carpet.

She caught herself as she felt herself sliding right off, her long auburn hair flipped over, causing her to raise one hand to brush it back, which resulted in her loosing her balance and toppling over onto the floor. Her right black stocking foot caught the coffee cup, sending that on a trajectory collided into the TV just as John Snow announced that another riot had broken out in London.

Through dripping coffee, totally unaware that he just had coffee splashed into his face, he turned and berated a spokesperson for inner London.

Upside-down with her legs over the coffee table, she blinked and muttered, "Oh, cool just ignore me then!" With a heavy sigh she rested her head on the edge of the sofa, looking through fronds of hair caught the black out line of her phone sticking up like the sentinel stone from 2001 a Space Odyssey in the large pot which held her giant rubber plant.

"Oh! So that's where you are!"

She slid her legs off the coffee table and with a few choice moans struggled to her feet, and walked round, side stepping the now well soaked in coffee stains that she knew would make her cleaning lady mutter and moan about in the morning. Bending down she plucked the still ringing phone, flipped it open and said, "Captain Lou Lou here!"

Thirty seconds later she snapped her wrist to close her mobile, not as good as on Star Trek, and she idly wondered why no one had thought of reproducing the gold grilled communicator?

With a gleam in her deep blue eyes, a smile that made grown men gooey she said, "Dinner!"

And began to sing slightly off key but with great euthasuim as she rushed to get ready.

"Sounds like a job for GOTH WOMAN!" and laughed as she ran into the bedroom. So it was for work, but at least she didn't have to cook. She hated cooking, cleaning, and far happier to dine out on the company's expense. Her bedroom was complete contrast to her living room; it was done in ten shades of amethyst, with cherry spotlights, and a duvet cover in deep maroon with silver stars, moons and planets covering a large four-poster bed with deep burgundy side curtains. In contrast to this she had a side dressing table that looked straight out of a theatre.

Only took her seconds to strip naked, throwing clothes in all directions with her usual care and almost took the eye out of her black and white cat, which had been snoozing on the mahogany bookcase.

He twitched and ducked when the bra twanged in his direction.

"Ooops sorry Mogs!"

Still giggling she picked up large silver backed brush and began to slowly untangle her hair.

The bulbs glowed white framing her face in the large mirror,

"And tonight Mathew I'll we be Cher! But without the facelift, boob job, tummy tuck, and remoulded arse!" She was a fan, but she knew that she didn't need anything done to improve the reflection she saw in the mirror. It was just a matter of what kind of persona would she play with tonight. How she was going to play the client to get the best deal for her firms up and coming Software Company. Being head programmer with a flair for selling anything was unique in the business.

She perused through the assorted make up jars, wigs, and prosthetics for that little change when she really wanted to be some one else. Having learnt from a boyfriend who had been a brilliant makeup artist in the states she could quite easily turn herself into virtually anybody, no matter the race. Without ever venturing to the knife. A good makeup could achieve anything.

Using a scrub sponge she cleaned off the days light makeup, and prepared the mix to be the foundation of her creative effort for the night.

ARC OF THE ANCIENTS

"Now then Moggs, don't sulk, you did duck!" The cat eyed her and yawned to show that he had forgiven her, then licked his paw and settled down to watch her. Lou Lou could see him in the reflection as she applied a light layer that turned her creamy milk white skin to a shade that was only slightly olive. Brushing lightly she used a suggestion of blush to highlight her cheekbones, and a little shadow to subtly alter the shape of her nose.

She had a narrow nose that flared out slightly, so with care she altered the line making it look slightly upturned and more defined in the areas that made her nose more even down the length and width.

While she worked she wondered if the client, Mr Atorn, whom she was due to have dinner with was going to be a good boy, or have to be put in his place. She knew she could be a terrible flirt but she didn't stand for any nonsense. She was confident that if he were more than playful she wouldn't hesitate to break something. Might lose the account but she wasn't for sell to anybody. Only her skill as a designer of some of the best game software to come out of the North for years was.

Her stomach rumbled as she took her time to finish, she hadn't realised how hungry she was. She had a slight case of heartburn as her stomach acid burbled and bubbled in impatience. Almost like her heart was on fire. She paused, the cat looked up, ears pricked, they looked at each other as a light wind fluttered in the room, making the bed drapes ripple.

Lou Lou didn't think she has left the window open. Her skin joined in with goose bumps, making her shiver. Her eye pencil halted as she slowly scanned the room reflected in front of her.

Nothing seemed out of place, that's when she noticed that her skin was flushing a deep pink, travelling from her heart out over her breasts up her neck to flush under the makeup of her face. Down her stomach, to her thighs and legs causing her feet to heat up and tingle.

It was like her temperture had risen by a degree or more. Then it slowly faded as she breathed again, not realising she had held her breathe.

The silence was broken by a screech and Moggs dived from the top of Bookcase and landed on the bed drapes, he clawed his way up and hid on the top canopy.

Lou Lou swivelled round on her chair, stood up and could only watch as a blue flame spat, sparkled then popped. A smell of ozone filled the room.

Then a light thud and a tinkle as something gold landed on the carpet.

"What on earth!" as she bent down, her breasts feeling heaver than normal, swayed as she gingerly reached to pick up, what appeared to be a diamond shaped golden broach.

It was warm, she felt light heady and giddy and almost fell on her bare bottom in shock. But she steadied herself more successfully then she had in the living room, and carefully sat back down and laid the object on her makeup table.

103

It was a flat diamond, with intricate lines and whirls with tiny writing, which she couldn't make out. They looked almost runic but she wasn't sure. It was only a half a centimetre thick and quite light, and about two centimetres long. It held Lou Lou mesmerised, all thoughts of dinner evaporated as she contemplated the wonder of how such a thing had come about.

"Where in hell did you come from?"

*   *   *

Bonus Item; A Short Story…

A CHRISTMAS TIME STORY
(A SANDAY WINTER TALE)

Jack's hand traced a pattern into the fine wet sand, the corner of the plastic bag with the tin of beans and slightly squashed loaf flapped furiously in the wind. His duffel coat, a size too big but warmer for it, had allowed the bag to slip free. He stopped his idle tracing and tucked the bag firmly into the back of his coat. He sat and stared at the crashing waves. The sea black and grey, boiled with tangled brown seaweed. The smell was strong, like something bad rotting away but tinged with the sharp tang of sea salt. He licked his lips tasting it. Could a day so close to Christmas be so grey? He looked up and down the lonely beach, rocks buried deep now in a blanket of brown seaweed. Not that it was called seaweed up here, but then he was finding that Orcadians had different words for things. He struggled to remember but gave it up.

Jack knew that he should be going home but it was end of term and was free enough to take his time. The school was one of things he liked, but he hadn't gotten used to the classes being so small. He was used to being ignored now attention was like a spot light every day. His mum said it would take some time to adjust. But he wondered if he would. He found going to Roadside shop in Lady scary, it was so dark inside and the people smelt so different. Not really bad and they all looked so wind swept and bundled. At least Jimmy the man who once owned the shop had a friendly round face. Not that Jack could understand what he said half the time so he nodded a lot and kept his own mouth firmly shut.

He wondered if his friends down south missed him, he certainly missed them, and the noise and colour of the city too. The air was unnaturally clean up here; funny he missed the constant smell of car fumes! Trouble was he was lonely, he hadn't made any new friends but then they had only been up on Sanday for a few weeks. His stomach still ached from the ferry crossings. The one to Stromness was bad enough but the Kirkwall to Loth was a much smaller ferry and as he hated roller coasters being tossed about on the sea was a never-ending nightmare. It made him sick just thinking about it. It just wasn't his home.

It was getting darker, the sea a constant noise seemed worse than ever and the cold wind made up his mind. Jack stood up, one booted foot on the carrier bag; he brushed the grey sand of his hands and jeans. Not that it did much good, and he gave up, picked up the bag and gently began to swing it back and forth as he walked up the beach.

He had yet to see anyone else on the beach, in the few weeks he had been on the island it seemed everyone went by car. There must be some people who just walked, but Jack had yet to see them. It just made it seem so empty.

Pulling down his woolly hat, which he hated but today was grateful for, even as the wind gusted and began to polish his face red. He bent into the wind and slowly followed the curve of the bay. He looked up occasionally to check where he was, looking out for the slip of sand that marked where he climbed down over the long grassy sand bank that marked the border of the beach.

In between the sandy bits he stepped carefully on the slippery carpet of seaweed, and the rubber like stalks, or branches of some alien tree. He remembered his Dad saying that some people on the Island collected them and dried them out up the beach. Mad! Obviously some strange island tradition. But then he thought they might have been the remains of some giant multi armed sea monster, smashed to bits by the sea. Or even that the locals came down at night armed with swords, cutting the arms off in a furious battle. He imagined they held torches in one hand as they fought side by side. Then in the morning came down to collect them. They obviously left some behind today! Maybe they had eaten their fill, and were lying with their hands resting on their big bellies, that made him smile.

He pretended he was a scout checking out the area for any more sea monsters, and crouched low spying out the lay of the land. He ran and jumped, then skidded to a stop as something ahead caught his eye. In the grey light he saw a dark hump in the distance. There were gulls ahead wheeling and climbing in the wind. Maybe another monster washed ashore? Caught up with the idea Jack crept closer, slowly he came to a rocky ledge that crossed the beach down to the sea. On his left above a crumbling cliff of sandy soil, a stone wall marked the back of a house. He didn't know who lived there, and climbing over the stone ledge he slipped down the other side. The dark smudge in the distance didn't move. But the birds above cried out and dived down, then glided just above the sandy cliff, following the contours of the land. It was amazing that they could do that even in this wind. Splashing through some pools, he crossed the stone and rocks until he reached the upper beach, and found a border of sand clean between the stones and the smelly seaweed. With the wind still in his face Jack couldn't make out what he had seen. There was more sand in the wind and it made his eyes itch and water. But he kept on, determined to find out what was ahead.

It was the smell that stopped him; it was so bad that he pulled his scarf up around his face. Trying to block the smell. It partly worked. The hump he had seen from a distance was now clear. Partly buried in the seaweed and sand was a grey black back of a sea creature. It was bigger than he first thought. He had never seen anything like it. Maybe those sea monsters were real after all! He backed off, and then stopped.

Deep gravel like voice said, " It won't hurt you, it's quite dead."

106

Startled Jack looked up, he looked around but there was no one there. Suddenly feeling very scared wishing he was safely home, thinking he should make a run for it. But only then realising that he had gone further along the beach than he had intended. Turning his head back and forth he didn't know what to do.

"Hey, up here!" There was a deep friendly laugh.

Jack looked up and there sitting on a small ledge of sand jutting out from the sand bank was a man. He had a big red woolly hat, a dark and light green coat. Brown knitted gloves holding a large twisted creamy yellow stick resting across his knees.

Through round dark glasses and a silver flecked black beard the man smiled and said," Look I don't bite, " a rumbling chuckle "I've eaten already today!"

Jack had a thought, looked down at the creature, saw what he took for bite marks, as the flesh was torn and took a step backwards.

"Oh yea, sure! "Remarked the strange man, and he was strange wearing such dark glasses in the depth of winter, "Obviously you think I eat whales!" The last said with such a grim expression that Jack almost bolted. But then the man laughed and for some reason it reminded Jack of Hagrid from the Harry Potter books. Not that the man was a giant of course, he was a lot shorter but as he was staring up at him he realised he wasn't scared any more and smiled back.

"That's better!" said the man. Swung his stick and using it to point at the rotting carcass added, "You never seen a dead whale before?"

Jack nodded his head no.

"Umm so you don't say much!"

Feeling brave Jack answered, "I'm not supposed to talk to strangers"

"Very wise!" Putting the stick back across his knees, the man "Well you better be off then."

Looking back down at the Whale, Jack thought it wasn't very big for a whale and feeling curious decided to say," Its not very big, I thought they were bigger."

The man scratched his beard and answered, "Okay, well it's only a baby and it's a lot bigger than you think, it's just buried under the sand. The storms must have been burying it for days. "

"Oh…" Was all Jack could think to say. While he stood trying to think of something else to say the Man stood up and carefully stepped down onto the stones. Leaning heavily on his stick to do so.

"Look I'm going to walk back home along the beach, you can walk with me if you wish."

He wasn't sure if he should and as the man began to walk away Jack made up his mind and decided if the man did anything odd then he could always run for it. He didn't think the man would catch him as he was leaning heavily on his stick and looked like it was an effort for him to even walk. Jack found it easy to keep pace, and feeling that the man was friendly looked up at him and asked, "Where did you get such a strange walking stick from?"

Pushing his glasses up with one hand, the man replied, "It's not a stick but a staff, and it was made for me by a very unique man who lives on another island in the Orkneys. His name is Jack."

"That's my name too!"

"Well, well, how curious, I wonder what the chances of that are?" The man stopped and added, "Okay Jack." And put out his hand. "A pleasure to meet you."

Feeling very grown up Jack shook the mans hand and said, "Pleased to meet you too." And grinned up at him. It was a change to be treated like an adult and not just a boy and Jack decided he liked this strange man.

Feeling comfortable as they carried on walking, asked, "Why do you wear dark glasses? Its not summer!"

The man laughed, and replied, "True, its not, and they are not dark glasses as such. They react to UV rays. And darken even on a grey day in winter like this."

"I thought they only reacted in bright sunlight."

"Well, now you know."

And that was how it began. Jack found himself talking more and more. The strange but friendly man listened to him and for the first time in ages he felt someone was *really* listening to him. His Mum and Dad were okay but they didn't always have time. As they walked along, the wind died down and the sky lightened. It was still crispy cold but Jack didn't mind as he was feeling that Sunday might not be so bad after all.

They had been walking for some time when the man suddenly stopped, leaned on his staff and looked down at Jack. "I have a feeling that I can trust you, would you like to see something curious?"

Jack's first thought was oh oh, my Mum warned me about people who said things like that! And took a few steps back. I just hope he's not a pervert!

The strange man must have seen something in his face and gave a tired sigh and said, "No wonder people believe there is no magic in the world, when our kids have to be taught to fear strangers." Then chuckled and added, "and I should choose my words more carefully!"

That made Jack smile with relief and the feeling of trust in this man hadn't changed and with confidence replied," So what did you mean?"

"Lets find a place to sit first then I'll tell you."

Within a short time they had walked into the second bay along the coast. Up ahead were the sand cliffs of Cata sands. On the other side was another bay and Lady village down the road. Jack lived in a small house up the right hand road just before the village. He realised that he had walked further then he had thought. He wasn't far from home. They had passed the golf course where the local doctor played in the afternoons. No one today though, Jack had heard his mum talk about that. It wasn't much of a golf course and often had sheep grazing on it. The wind had dropped even more, and soon they had the sand cliffs to their left. About midway the man stopped, finding a place just under the cliff sat on the sand. Jack sat down beside him, he watched as the man struck the staff into the sand. Surprisingly it went deep, about a third of the way down. The sea was still rough but white crests on the waves were a lot softer.

In a clear soft but deep voice the strange man began, "This Island has had people living on it for thousands of years, many different people have come and gone. Now we are in a time that new people like you and I have come. Newcomers as some still like to say, but just as their ancestors were once, so we join the long line going back far into time. There have been some who have realised that this island has a special quality that has managed to survive even into this time. The spirit of this island is still strong."

He paused and Jack saw that that the man's glasses had cleared, and he could see that he had deep brown eyes with flecks of gold and they shone as he continued;

"And if you know how, you can talk to the island and in turn reach others." He winked and smiled at Jack.

Now Jack wondered if this man might just be a bit mad! But then for some reason he thought that if Harry Potter, who he had always felt, ever since he read the first book, was a real person and his friends down south had thought him a little strange in the head when he mentioned that, was this any different? He continued to search those eyes for the truth of this feeling and smiled to himself. Well if you took away the beard, he could be a grown up version of Harry Potter for all he knew. Some people have said that JK Rowling is really Hermione and he guessed that this man was about the same age. Not that he was that good at judging the ages of old people. And there is a faint scar on his forehead in the right place. And they might even know each other!

Caught up with that idea he said, "Have you ever read Harry Potter?"

The man chuckled and said, "Of course! I know about Harry..."

"Your name wouldn't be Harry?" Asked Jack.

The man just laughed, but kindly and said," Look shall we continue or do you want to talk about Harry Potter?"

Hoping he hadn't spoilt anything he quickly said, "No, go on."

Smiling the man reached into his pocket and took out a harmonica. "Now watch out to sea and listen carefully Jack."

He did as he was told and watched the sea as the man began.

At first nothing much seemed to happen, just the sound of the sea mixed with the sound of the man playing a strange tune on his harmonica. It reminded Jack of his Grandfather who had suddenly died the year before. He had a memory of his Irish uncle playing on his harmonica. That made him feel warm and then he noticed that the sky was darkening. Clouds came rushing in and as the tune changed in pitch it began to snow. Big white fluffy snow falling on the sand. His attention was drawn to the staff. It was glowing! Soft white gold light flickered over it and it seemed to be singing!! This was amazing! A hand gently touched his shoulder and he felt himself turned back to look at the sea. It was as flat as a pond and then breaking through he saw nine humps, then nine tails rise out of the water. Whales! He knew they were whales! He had seen them on TV. The tails or Flukes as he knew was the proper name splashed down and then he heard them.

It was like nothing he could have imagined. The sound filled his head, making his heart swell to bursting point as joy filled him so completely. For a moment he felt like he was deep in the sea, the sound of family and belonging brought tears to his eyes. He didn't think it was possible to feel what he was feeling. For a moment he felt like the island was holding him up, a deep female presence wise and powerful welcomed him to her heart and with a kiss like his mothers on his brow felt a breeze bring him home to himself.

The island sang, the whales sang, the sea sang, and his heart sang with the joy of it. Then it faded, he found himself standing alone on the beach. No sign of the strange man, or the whales and the sea had returned to white angry waves.

Was it real? What had happened? He looked into the grey day, and saw that it was white and the snow was falling still. He didn't notice the cold or that he was still holding the bag with the tin of beans and the partly squashed loaf. He didn't notice that he had walked home.

Until the door burst opened and his mum was hugging him and laughing that he had certainly taken his time. And what a relief he was home safely. Lights from the tree, the smell and colour of the flames of the dark peat fire as he was wrapped in a blanket and a hot mug of tomato soup were placed into hands.

From a far distance a voice chuckled and a whisper said, "Merry Christmas Jack." They didn't ask why he smiled all the time through the holidays or why he no longer moaned about living on Sanday. He couldn't explain he was truly home...[14]

THE END

---

[14] *For Jack and the people of Sanday- First published in the SANDAY SOUND Jan 2003*

INTERLUDE!

Rules For Being An Alien in a Human Body

You will receive a choice of body. Short, wide, tall, thin, but pick your type wisely! Be Happy with it! Its your home away from your own skin!!!

You can pick your own cool colour. But not Blue, Purple, or Bright Green! As they are not acceptable yet because of some strange colour pred-juices! Yeh we don't get why they do that either!

Where you can park your scout craft. Becareful that you remember where you parked! Reports have come in that some jokers among you keep using govermently parking spaces - Its not funny.... oh and the Whitehouse Lawn is not optional!

Remember that your craft is trans dimensional - And become invisible to the human eye - So remember to place a marker that your human eyes can see!! You can't change your eyes you know!

You will learn lessons. You are enrolled on a planet called earth. Each day you will be confronted by great oddness and wish fervently that you were back on board the mothership!

There are loads mistakes to be had, in fun filled lessons. Growth is a process of trial and error: experimentation is lots of fun. But becareful how you grow all your bits! Otherwise you may become an exibit!

Leave Cows, horses, sheep etc alone. Some wise cracker has thought fit to nick a few - and take away certain bits - yes wer know the humans do it - But they don't generally leave the evidence behind them! Our reputaion is bad enough without that!

A skin is for life not just for christmas. There was a report that some of you are beaming a few aboard your ships so you can change your skins - please remember your manners and Don't do it.

A lesson does not end. Becareful of the indigenous lifeforms as they will teach you until you explode!. If you are alive after this then you will have learned your lesson!

There is no better than 'Here.' ' When your 'There' is over here" then you have jumped through a time flaw - So make sure your "here is over here" a lot less confusing then being over "there

Others are merely mirrors of you. If you have chosen someone elses skin then give it back and hope they didn't notice!

What you make of life is up to you. You have all the tools and resources you need. Emergency call to the mothership is prohibited unless you are have some nice take aways that we will all enjoy.What you do with the leftovers is up to you.

The answer lies within you. The answer to life's questions lie inside you. Yes you are an Alien trying to be a human. All you need to do is to look in the mirror and realise its a mask - if you don't like it then you should have picked more wisely you fool! Listen and trust the sublime messages on Alien F.M. The music is cool too!

Do not abuse your position. Its come to my attention that some of you are using your greater awareness to alter the flow of this worlds time line - You are not there to become president, dictator or Queen mother- and you know whom I speak off!

And its not a computer game. You only have one life , one skin, and No there is no "save" or "Load" option! and no cheats either - even though some jokers keep posting walkthrou's! - Its your life they can't have a walkthru other than their own you dolts!

If you forget any of this. Well its no picnic so you'll have to make it up as you go along - you have been warned! So Becareful Out there! "$^{\Omega}$

$^{\Omega}$ Extracts Transcribed from the idiot's guide of *Aliens in Human clothing* ©Copright 2000 held by the Galactic council. Permission granted by the supreme ruler oh doggy like Martin. A Enticknap.

This Second Half of this works is Dedicated to
All the friends who are memories deep in my heart
Many who are reflected in the poetry here.

Also to my Mum and Dad who never realized what they had
started!

And my Uncle Alan and Auntie Jean,
Who were more important for a memory than they knew.
Rest in peace.

And Finally to my two Nans, rest in peace,
So different but not forgotten.

Acknowledgements must be made to
Christine, Keely, Zoe and the rest of the family, Linda, Jim, Katherine,
Angelina, Yvana and the rest of the family whose friendship for twenty
years brought me hope and light in some of my darker days, who
without the love and support I might never have made it through.
Never forgetting those others that made the first part of my life more
than just a little interesting! With Fond memories, Julia, Carol, Helen,
Pip, Karen, Peter, Tim, Steven, Martin M, Fiona, Debbie, Claire, Susan
C, Heidi, Maxine, Debbie G, Tracy, Jane, Nicole, Ann W, Maria B,
Karen W and to anyone else whose name I've forgotten!

My First Collection of Poems 1978 – 1987

THE CIRCLE OF LIFE COLLECTION

THE LAST ROSE

The beauty of this dark red rose,
Shines out, radiating; pleasure, happiness,
And love to all those around this,
Dark Red Rose.

Like the red rose, you shine out,
From the crowd, pink cheeks, dark eyes,
You are my Red rose,
Velvet petals like your skin,
Smooth, warm and hopeful.

You are my last rose,
That will stay in my heart forever,
Now the time has come to say goodbye,
To you, my Dark Red Rose.

Written In 1978   Aged 14

For Carol

CAT

Black and white tattered cat,
Wanders a field, prowling,
Pouncing on its pitiless prey,
 That slick cat, when all,
Is dark, sits on my window ledge,
Meowing; " Its cold out here! "
The window creaks, that cat pounces,
Lands skilfully on my bed,
Curls up and rest its head and sleeps.

Morning bright but early, birds singing,
The wind whistling in the trees,
A faint cry of a cat reaches my ears,
There, by the windowsill,
I open the window,
Like a streak of light she is gone.

I go out later and there is that cat,
 Tapping softly on the kitchen window,
Her eyes gleaming bright,
Caught by the fire of sunlight,
Her hunger reaches me, I open the window.

Those powerful jaws with razor sharp teeth,
And pink tongue nestled in her jaw,
She devours her meal and disappears once more,
To hunt by the light of day,
Then to the night a glorious sleep,

A reflection of day into night,
This dream of a prey who dies, squealing,
Brave noble mouse who dies by the claw,
Red flesh tattered and torn,
That mighty creature the cat plays,
 With pitiless mouse forever more.

Written on 31/10/79   Aged 15

For a Cat

115

THE QUESTION OF LIFE

There is life and there is death,
There is happiness and hatred,
But what has life to do with me,
 Women may laugh and men may cry,
But Why? Is this life?

A baby is born and a baby dies,
 There was laughter and sadness,
 But what has life to do with me,
Men may die, would the women cry?
But Why? Is this life?

A life was saved but a life dies,
 There was happiness and mourning,
 But why do they live and die?
Men may fight while the women mourn,
But Why? Is this life?

There is no life and no death,
Happiness and hatred, joy or tears,
They do not exist, but for you,
There may be realities and illusions,
But why? Is this life?

I do not need life or death, I can't die,
I can't feel happiness or sorrow,
But I exist, so do you, so why is there life?
Men may destroy and women give life,
But for me why should there be?
For I'm just the dust at your feet....

Written on 11/1/80   Aged 16

COUNTRY SIDE

The essence of life begins in the countryside,
Where trees grow and wild flowers bloom,
A place which shows more beauty,
When observed by country sunlight,
Like no other place can.

When day dawns and birds sing,
That's when the day begins,
As life brings more life,
Cows moo, dogs bark and cockerels crow,
The small church rings its bells as life awaken.

The roar of the tractor and human voices,
As men, women and children agree,
What a lovely morning,
The day has started once again,
Showing that the village and countryside belong together.

When the sun sets, the insects awaken,
Crickets stir, bats fly out,
The old women across the road stirs,
And goes to bed as the village grows silent,
While the countryside gets ready for another day.

Written on 30/8/80   Aged 16

TODAY TIME ENDS

The things we promise to accomplish end,
The hopes and fears will die,
The time of day and night will end,
Sorrow, grief and mourning will begin,
The seasons of life and accomplishment,
Will finally come to an end.

The time bearers will be forfeit of life,
The lives on earth will die,
Human and animal alike as time wills the end,
The things which will matter to time,
Is the spectacle of injustice and justice,
As all comes to an end.

People will stop and time will be destroyed,
So that life will not follow,
Body will exist but will remain hollow shell,
This is the meaning of a trapped earth,
With none to care for the welfare,
Of this hallowed place in time.

The final accomplishment of Man,
Is to find the consequences of the end of time,
Will the end accomplish the mean?
No! The time will end from the start,
And Man shall become the victim and not the victor.

Written on 29/12/80 Ages 17

LIFE

There are moments in life when life is wealth,
And a beauty is a real part that exists,
There are people that bring sparkle and enjoyment,
They enrich and bring forth happiness.

Beauty, richness and a symbol of life,
That glows warmth and is all that matters,
Life is a form of existence that fills still,
Creatures with expression and a voice,
Something to add - Good or Evil.

118

ARC OF THE ANCIENTS

Life changes and shapes people and creatures,
When young people or old show life,
They bring real enjoyment and laughter,
They are the life that shows their humanity.

The hopes of life that it brings is a part,
That all people show when they are capable of laughter,
Two very special lives effect mine,
One more than the other but equal in effect,
For the colours of life they have added.

Written on 25/12/82 Aged 19

For Christine K and her Mum Anne

THOSE PEOPLE!

They who are - they are,
They try to be different from what they are,
To blend with the rest but with thoughts inside their heads;
We are so superior to so many,
They try to enjoy themselves but many can't,
As they force themselves on others,
And reject so many.

Ignorance is the master of their race,
The multitudes who are,
This blindness leads to great unhappiness,
And a tragedy as they are - who they are.

Those people who populate this planet,
Their dreams are so many,
Of material gain - in wealth of power,
Are the predominant of them all,
Of those who are - they are.

They try to have more than their fellow beings,
The battle commences and a struggle for their very existence,
Becomes the factor and result of the initial stage,
Of who they are - they are.

They welcome you with one hand,
And then stab you in the back with other,
The tendency of those who are,
Dig it in as far as possible with great relish,
Those people who are - what they are.

If a question is to be answered,
Of all who claim to be,
Are they who they want to be,
Or are they the lie of who they are?
Those people who know the truth can see,
When they shed the shell and find,
The true understanding of who they really are to be.
And not a bloody politician!

Written on 6/4/83 Aged 19

THE LONELY

The lonely are the lonely,
They feel much they want very little,
They see what they need and when they see it,
It's at a distance beyond comprehension and reach.

To be there lonely,
The wanting of another human soul,
To care for them for what they are and nothing more,
This develops to become the force of their lives,
With some it drives and others it buries,
And with a force that can overwhelm,
Their very essence of being.

ARC OF THE ANCIENTS

Hope is a factor that erodes with time,
It crumbles and dies an agonizing death,
Pity they do not need,
A falsity is fuel to the fire,
And another nail in the coffin.

The loneliness of the heart,
To love to feel loved,
To search for that one person,
In the crowd you may dwell,
The lonely spirit that cannot fill that,
Awesome ache with other people just being around.

In deepest depth, down in the heart of your soul,
No peace of mind can be found,
On an horizon of hope it may appear,
This love which could be shared.
But it cannot be reached until that other,
Hand decides that their love is for you,
For your hands to finally meet.

But when that horizon is too far,
Where no warm hands are there to be grasped,
This is when the tears do fall,
Spilt upon that lonely ground,
Each drop being the pain of life itself.

Written on 6/4/83 Aged 19

CHRISTINE

You are the one that I know and you are special,
These words are a message expressing my feelings for you,
The beauty you are and the light you bring,
To the dark recesses of my mind,
The ache and yearning for you are,
They exist - these and many more come forth,
Expressing my love for you,
You are the one in my heart Christine.

Those eyes express great feeling and passion,
They sparkle, shine, radiate, reflections that can be seen,
As they ricochet across the eyes becoming light,
Your eyes capture my soul and you have me,
As when your eyes alight upon mine own,
You are the one in my eyes Christine.

Every moment, every time you move those lips,
They capture the imagination,
The words you speak, like crystal are clear,
Reflecting a music all your own,
You speak no words of love to me,
Your heart evades me, its beyond my reach,
At this moment in time,
But you are the one who's lips,
Will always speak beauty,
To all who hear you Christine.

This poem is my message to the girl who captured me,
You have my heart in those fair hands,
Whose touch also evades mine,
Their warmth I'll not have as your hands clasp another,
This touch of your hands,
The instrument of your expression,
Those that you touch you melt,
You have the touch of life that can give pleasure,
My darling Christine.

But even though I may feel the pain of love rejected,
Of my heart that threatens to break,
And of tears that may fall,
At least I'll always have the colours,
That have made my life worth living,
In knowing you Christine.

This is the end of my poem for you,
Your beauty is you, those eyes that are yours is you.
The lips that are made for kisses,
Sweet, warm and hopeful should never go cold,
They can be used for expressing love, passion, feeling,
That pleasure has not been mine,
Your touch that makes the touch,

ARC OF THE ANCIENTS

The hands the easiest link I know,
The most important thing of all that needs no other words,
Is you - mind, body and soul,
Christine.

Written on 9/4/83 Aged 19

For Christine K

ME

I am ME, the person, the man I am,
This body is mine, the time is now,
I live, I breathe, the air I breathe I live,
This is the person who knows much yet knows little,
Life is my Knowledge.

I know that life is life that brings pain, sorrow, hurt,
The pang of life to be fulfilled to the end,
I am ME in all these things,
That also embrace, happiness, joy, pleasure, life.

Much to go on and see to feel that life is for ME,
To know the meaning is to understand,
That we will find our true selves,
The purest thing is truth, the positive, the power,
The will to live.

I am not understood by the people I exist with,
They will find there is more to ME,
Then they will ever know,
The life is my will, the people my knowledge,
The end is the will that can be.

The force that grows to wait, to nourish,
And be fulfilled to grow stronger,
This force is being prepared to unleash unto the world!
The life which is ME will be a force,
That when its ready will explode and change the world,
For I am ME,
The meaning of ME is the knowledge of life itself.

Written on? /5/83 Aged 19

YOU

There are times when much is needed,
The many ways in which you the person,
The ever undying beauty, the real explosive,
It is YOU.

The only person ever to install peace unto me,
The inner most fabric of my mind,
Is the never ending joy which I feel,
When I lay in your arms,
It is YOU.

The time is now and where are we going,
This is a question for all,
But its meant for us,
Well she, the woman, the pure and wonderful person,
It is YOU.

These seeds are young and if they are to grow,
Understanding, patience and love is needed,
This I say, my words are true,
For when we become one but two,
It is right, it is YOU.

ARC OF THE ANCIENTS

The time is now in life, your seeds are there,
Be patient then they will grow,
This I feel and I know that you are real,
I am and you are,
It is YOU.

Two people in life, friendship and love could be ours.
But promises are made for breaking,
So we will make none,
For peace and truth will prevail,
Thank you for being,
It is YOU.

Written on 1/8/83 Aged 19

For Lydia

FREEDOM

To be free, when the mind can find peace,
The body free from tension,
This I say unto you, all who yearn to be free,
When the shackles of life are thrown off,
The pressure thrown clear,
Clarity of thought shall become,
And body and mind become one,
This you will see and the truth shall become yours.

Real freedom can be found,
Where nature lies and roams the earth,
The creatures which aren't human are free,
Their lives are free and they are the true ones,
They know and understand,
But Man is the shackled one by his own design.

To leave, to get up and go,
To explore and find,
To seek out through nature you must go,
In harmony and love you should give,
For hostility breeds nothing but pain,
And freedom will be denied,
For the lesson to be learnt,
To soar free with the birds,
Understand and you will find what you seek,
The eyes that are closed must be opened.

Freedom is what all men fight for,
Through all time they have fought,
But yet it has been denied,
For he shackles his life by lies,
And no peace shall he find,
For freedom belongs to the creatures that aren't human,
And not for Man until he learns to be kind,
Understanding, patient, compassionate and to love all,
That he lives with.

This I dream, this I seek, my freedom,
For while I stay in the confines of humanity,
I shall not find and be denied,
For its the fate of all Men who live,
Until the day is ripe and the time is ready,
Then will is done and man shall find his freedom,
And peace shall be his,
For the price is high and the risk is great,
For the truth is the answer and freedom is given.

Originally written 5/8/83 Aged 19

ARC OF THE ANCIENTS

SUMMER NIGHT

This night is all nights, dark and peaceful,
Those that roam at night along the dark streets,
The cool welcoming breeze, refreshing them,
On this warm summer night.

The night folk are awaken, in their element,
People who find magic in this night,
As they walk home from an evening with friends,
Who may stop to touch skin upon hot skin,
Of thirst that is quenched and hunger satisfied,
Let it be known this night is for lovers,
On this hot summer night.

After the day of hot stifling heat,
Of office workers who cannot breathe,
And fainting children in the streets,
The coolness is welcome,
As this curtain of magic night that descends,
Is a friend to us all,
On this welcome summer night.

It seems we owe them much,
For dreams are formed and promises are made,
Secrets are told and love is woven in the stars.
For all we treasure,
On this golden summer night.

The nights we make are own for a brief time,
And as dawn comes to say goodbye,
We see our wishes come true,
The stillness and tranquility are sweetness,
Of our special sighs,
They we treasure all winter long,
For on cold nights we remember these fond memories,
That return us to those enduring summer nights.

Written on 6/8/83 Aged 19

LOVE AND HOPE

Its sometimes hard to say how I feel,
Words can stumble on feelings,
That are so important for me to convey to you.
Among the grey stones of lost words,
I now dwell, my heart is so heavy,
That it brings me to my knees,
The cry of hope that needs to say,
Is caught in a web of confusion,
As you walk by and it seems like forever,
That I have been frozen to this spot,
Watching you for an eternity,
As you walk on your way.

Your smile, the twinkle in your eyes,
Pin me securely like a butterfly to a board,
How can I, a mere mortal reach up to you,
A goddess in every way but name,
So I am here, a hunger in my heart,
The heat of my passion for you,
Cooled only by the tears that fall,
As you fade further away.

Is it a mountain I must climb?
To reach the summit and declare my love?
Will you hear me or will all be lost in the wind,
But I, as it will always be, will fail,
As I feel the wind rush by as I slowly fall,
Forever it will be in love with you,
So certain is the pain and joy as I tumble down,
Hoping that you will be there to catch me,
Your vibrant embrace to hold me close,
And not the harsh cold surface of stone,
For my ultimate destiny.

A dream you remain,
No flesh and blood of warm womanhood,
No love filled laughter,

ARC OF THE ANCIENTS

For you will have to remain to me,
The purest goal that needs to be broken,
For a goddess on her pedestal cannot reach me,
While I support that immortal stone.

When I can climb from my knees,
Lift the veil of worship from my eyes,
Then and only then may I find the self worth,
To hold you tight, to love you rather than cold stone,
But until that day you will always fill my dearest dreams.

Written on 22/10/83 Aged 19

For Billie Ann

A WORLD FOR CHILDREN

The world hears from the beginning,
A shattering cry as they enter our world,
Taking their first breath,
Of This their future world.

A place for them to learn and grow,
Of peace and understanding,
Of all the beauty in the colours,
Of a secure and free world.

An illusion I can see,
For there is too much pain for them,
Of broken lives and darkened hearts,
Making unfit children for an unfit world.

Too much sadness, no hope,
Bequeathing an eternal darkness,
Upon atomic dust they might walk,
From the generation that exist in this our world.

A plea to you all - those Mums and Dads,
Look for a better understanding,
As you guide them with tolerance,
And most of all love in your world.

Don't abuse the position you hold,
Learn from your mistakes,
So the torch you pass isn't faulty,
Please I beg of you in lighting their world.

Teach your children better,
Help them along their difficult path,
Don't block but understand your children,
As they learn of your world.

This world has a duty to the children,
Don't forget they walk in your footsteps,
And inherit the world you construct,
So they can reach for the dream of a better world.

Don't leave it for them to say,
Too much hurt was inflicted - Too many broken children,
Too many shattered hearts and broken promises,
Too many eyes crying tears in an unloved world.

If that is your desire and you allow it to continue,
Then the world will end with a cry of despair,
That will ring out for all eternity,
From all the World's Children.

Written on 20/5/84 Aged 20

DARKNESS

We exist in a cloud of darkness,
All living in a dark age,
The Earth in hiding,
Behind a black and stifling cloak,
The light left struggling,
To penetrate upon this world of ours.

This I say - all you have to do to see,
Is to look around you,
Intolerance is wreaking our land,
The destruction is making the Earth tremble,
And crumble around us,
Leaving the sky to weep the blackest tears.

Murder, pain and sorrow of all,
As ignorance is strong as a inflexible wall,
The people left helpless,
Their lack of understanding is a wandering blindness,
With no feeling and no reason to live,
So lost but hoping to be found.

Down deep inside they want to journey,
To find their way to the light,
But the voice of the people is not true,
Stifling growth, learning, love and truth,
We see it but no comprehension exists to fight it,
As the Darkness becomes complete.

Written on 20/5/84 Aged 20

QUEST

To a world of today is the answer of tomorrow,
The answer is not from a world question,
The answer is held here - Now!
But where to look!
Into myself could be the answer...

The channeling of thoughts that go far beyond,
The normal bounds of our minds,
To travel deep to find an answer to the question,
But without some outside aid,
The path is difficult and not easily passed,
To the center of all minds knowledge.

We give up and the answer we need is not given,
The change does not come,
The fulfillment of dreams remain dreams,
And only Dreams....

The metamorphosis of the being must be achieved,
Or a waste is the result,
The final outcome through a pathway,
Held out in the realms of antiseptic wards,
At 9.00 o'clock tomorrow the start,
The trail - The result!!

The phoenix rising from the ashes,
The new, the complete metamorphosis has occurred,
The result shall be determined,
Or failure to find the path,
The question begs an answer!
A mystery of nine months must be solved...

A feeling - An awareness!
Of events at the time of the year,
A feeling of certain knowledge,
Something was going to happen!
But what ?
I waited and waited,
It grew stronger and stronger,
Then a date of an event,

ARC OF THE ANCIENTS

Could the answer lay there ?
Near the time of importance,
The answer has possibilities for here...

Tomorrow I shall find if events are going,
To be played out here!
Tomorrow a answer to an answer,
A question of the end to a 20 year Quest...

Written on (11.36PM) 17/10/84 Aged 20

THE GROUP

This group of people gathered here,
To talk and listen,
On words that are written,
On paper that tells of work and skill.

Of time spent on many a night with mobile pen.
Of faces of expression that show animation,
Of thoughts and deeds,
Of voices of learning,
That pass on their knowledge,
Of this I see - I listen.

Of stories told and words that are added,
To tell of things to encourage,
To add a comment constructive,
They help to gather words together,
For the example for us all.

I gather their words and inspiration,
To write a small poem,
That tells of an experience,
That makes we come back,
To listen and enjoy,
So my pen may write once more.

Written on (2.57AM) 6/2/85 Aged 21

For the Scribblers.

EPIC

The plains of time go through the circle of light,
To find the source to see through the end,
We are light sources and dark sources,
The event we are about to witness,
Shall inflame the lights of all reason,
To enlighten ~o the souls of all creation,
To this we shall witness.

The Epic is about to begin,
The stage is set....
For we are about to transform this world.
The Editors are to come forward,
To tell that they will begin to edit life,
How? Why?
Two questions - two answers,
 That make even more questions.

As the flames of light and wisdom enlighten,
Upon the souls of the people of this world,
As they move through their lives,
The changes shall become more pronounced to them,
Effecting their life patterns.
A start and a beginning,
The clocks are beginning the Countdown...

Written on10/4/85 Aged 21

COUNTDOWN

The energy from the stars,
 Race to the planet Earth,
It will bring new sights for us to see,
Changing the night sky,
A firework display,
Like nothing before witnessed by Man,
Only at the beginning,
 Was such an event witnessed,
 By more comprehending eyes.

We gaze in awe - We shall gain and lose,
Remember there is always a price to pay,
When the vision widens,
Thus the great gathering shall begin,
From every corner of the world,
They shall travel,
To meet at the most important place on Earth.

This is the place where all energy comes to rest,
Where they meet and touch,
Mingle and flow and gain new strength,
For power is found in new waters,
From where it will blossom,
Like a flower in spring,
Pure white energy that will pulsate,
 Glowing like a new star.
 Which has a Destiny...

Written on 15/4/85 Aged 21

DESTINY

This power which is contained,
In the energy of souls,
That gathers in many forms,
To encircle the light as it becomes known,
Changing the structure of particles,
 Atoms that fuse to bring forth life,
In variation in sight and sound,
This will have a name that it will be known,
The reason it comes to pass.

The process begins to slow,
Actively reducing the pulsating light,
Which begins to understand,
As changes from the purity of white light,
Bring it into the spectrum of itself,
 In all the glory of colour,
 That shapes the imagination.

This Epic that continues to its Destiny,
That exist as a new life form,
Is but a prelude to a greater event,
For mankind this ultimate change,
From the most restricted form of life,
To the free most of them all,
When minds loosen from their bonds,
 The gift they shall receive,
 Will let mind speak to mind.

Its name will be known,
For what it is,
 The truth of all,
As Man knows and all he doesn't.
 An interlude to consider,
The nature of this truth.

Its time,
The pulsating colour becomes mobile,
 It gathers its strength to depart,
To fly to its goal,
They look on in sadness,

ARC OF THE ANCIENTS

As it gracefully ascends to the heavens,
To kiss the stars,
They have given and thus been changed,
No longer a lost whisper,
But with one voice they do speak,
A thought that can be heard,
Through out the World,

The destination of truth is a journey,
Of finding new worlds,
Of souls who do not have the truth,
Of life to be born,
Then when the heavens of a new earth,
Sees the fireball light their sky,
Then they will have a Destiny.

.... For Destiny bequeaths Destiny.

Written on 17/4/85 Aged 21

ZXCUBVCX

The words we speak in chatter,
As mouths work on forming words,
Of a language that tells us what?
What do we mean when we communicate?
Is it to pass the time of life?
To use spare moments of time?
To waste in idle talk?
With the end result of nothing?!
Nothing to learn and nothing to give!!

Zxcubvcx - means absolutely nothing to you,
But in ways it is what you say when you talk,
Making conversation of nothing,
We waste and misuse a way of communication,

137

That is open to question because of its misuse,
To find a way of talking,
That does not become open to misuse,
By the people attempting to use it.

Words can be a powerful weapon that can change worlds,
Make or break a person in their rise to power,
A politician - The animal that has become master,
Of the meaningless words - the ultimate misuse,
Of a form of communication.

There is a lesson to be learnt in there,
Use it if you can find it!
You may become Prime minister or a new Messiah!!
Zxcubvcx - is either a political lie,
Or a new power of understanding...

Written on 30/4/85 Aged 21

Nan

To you I write a poem,
So written words can say of the feelings,
Not easily expressed by a spoken word,
The love you gave will always remain,
And be cherished.

My Nan, you gave so much that,
Is not yet fulfilled in the eyes of others,
The mother of my mother,
That gives me the time to write these words,
So I wait in your house of word of you,
As you lay in the hospital bed.

My heart reaches out to you,
My spirit aches to comfort,
As you grip onto life,
So you fight for the peace you wish.

ARC OF THE ANCIENTS

My mother, uncle and aunt are at your side,
And the love they give to you surrounds you,
Protects you in your last hours,
As your grip begins to loosen,
Like the sleep you have fallen into,
May there be no more pain,
For you to suffer.

I came so I may say goodbye,
And as your hand gripped mine,
In a last farewell,
I shall always remember you,
In the ring that you gave to grandad,
Then gave to me,
As it reminds me of grandad,
It will remind me of you both,
Together again never to part.

Written on 6/7/85 (3.18 AM) Aged 21

For My Nan (Jones) who died at 3.16 am 6/7/85

POWER

To all who believe in the stories of old,
Of myth and legend,
To the furthest reaches of our future,
Of worlds not bound by our reality,
They are steeped in the blood of power,
The struggle of good and evil.

The mystic battles of war,
Of a land not ready for the evil it's spawned,
But where Elves, dwarves and centaurs,
And other mythical beings prepared to fight,
Against Trolls, goblins and giants,

And darker powers,
When the good is out numbered by the evil hordes,
There comes a shining spark to redress the balance.

Of one soul that takes up the banner,
For a quest of power,
Be it through the power of rings or sword,
That blazes with white light,
And the power of a mind to harness,
The good to destroy evil,
While the dark lord prepares to crush,
And bring the Dark Age to the land.

When power is tapped of a will of evil,
Power corrupts,
It consumes all light and a dark lord is born,
To ravish and rape the land,
And poison all waters.

In the age before man,
When magic was the tool,
The creatures of magic roamed the land,
The heroes were created and legends were born.

Then they began to pass and their numbers dwindled,
Then man came and the age of in-between,
When man knew of magic and the power of mind,
And nature that could bring beauty and horror.

Then the magic died from the land,
When belief turned to disbelief,
The creatures of magic disappeared and withdrew,
To places where man could never venture.

Through the age of man the power of old,
Sparkles only briefly through the shroud of grey,
Only brought through by a rare mind or through
Writing of stories and tales,
When the power of good and evil come once more.

As the age of man comes to a close,
It will only have one tale to tell,
Of battles and a war that had its roots,

ARC OF THE ANCIENTS

In the old magic.

A dark lord that returned and used the very fabric of man,
To conquer and destroy,
But where his power was of old,
He used the evil of men to do his bidding.

When a world is blind and lets the evil spread,
An old rule comes into play,
The light did shine to bring a mind of war,
And a power that led a world to war and won.

The dark lord was destroyed and the light,
Of the man faded and became history.

So as mankind comes to its final chapter,
And the world changes once again,
And a new age begins,
As he climbs out of the ashes,
He will find that his kind,
Will have spawned new races.
That will take the names of the old,
To rename the new,
And a new and far greater world of power will be born,
And then the fantasy becomes the reality.

There will always be a sword of light,
To fight the darkness.

Written on 8/9/85 (4.55 AM) Aged 21

FEELINGS

To feel life is to live life,
More in the way of us the human race,
And not the robotic illusion that we use,
To fool all around us but which make,
Us the biggest fool of all.

141

To take it for granted the emotions,
We have and you risk losing them for a time,
Then the loss you will see but the emotion,
Is numb – removed from the picture,
To only look on at the world,
Around and the people you live with.

So alone you become because you can only play,
In emotion to copy by force,
What you think you should feel,
Then the day may dawn,
If you are lucky and realize that you don't,
Think to feel you just feel,
The thoughts come on reflection.

Control may start you on a road,
That leads to a wall which blocks,
Your every move so you trap yourself,
And the road you approach alone.

When you can start to take that wall apart,
Brick by brick a little feeling flows through,
To encourage your effect in restoring yourself,
To yourself – but the hardest brick of all,
Is to let go then the wall will fall,
And you are free once again.

A philosophy of man grew in the past history,
To confuse and blind our fellow beings,
To deny is to control the emotional flow,
Is to be a killing machine.
Some will break and drown in,
The emotional lake they have denied,
Others will become the spectre of the fullest horror,
Of every human of our race.

Life demands a rule you may say,
Control is to save our sanity,
But I say you play on dangerous ground,
That will one day give way beneath your feet.

If you must use your emotions to control yourself,

ARC OF THE ANCIENTS

Go with the flow but if it flows to danger,
Then turn the stream another way,
But if it is denial then the feelings begin to die,
And so do you.

Written on 19/1/86 Aged 22

INSPIRATION

With every stroke of the brush a little love flows through,
Every strand of hair vibrated into life,
The attention brings the passion of a careful hand,
Transforming to other worlds,
To be affected across eons of time and space,
The worlds feel the cool air with the inner warmth blowing swiftly,
Which can only bring delight.

From small actions come the events of great meaning,
That can be more important than anything yet imagined,
In this space in time.

Like the ripples on the surface of a lake,
One step leads to outer worlds,
In the hair, in the head, to the body,
To the person, then through to worlds,
And far into the universe itself.

Waves of an ocean brings you the voice
Of the world, a way to communicate like the wind,
That brushes the sea as in that hand in movement,
Of grace captured in a moment of love.

Inspiration from the small can be what changes,
Every life and though the eyes of an outside entity,
Can reveal what is hidden from the eyes in the blind of spirit.

Can there be more in the play of mutual sprits,
That twirl in a spiral,
To heights reaching to the peak in the expression,
Of a voice of the free.

Written on 26/7/86 (11.30 PM) Aged 22
For Stevie and cathy

"A LARGE POT OF TEA – THANK YOU"

Sitting in a teashop sipping a cup of tea,
The things I see, I listen, I wait,
Many times I have waited by the sea,
The ages in-between,
The multi-woven pattern of the alien race,
Called human they say.

Clank, bang, chatter, crash, the sounds,
Of a song?

Music made from shadows grasping on the edge of reality,
Brown eyes peering in on the scene,
Pretty face behind the counter,
Serving her fellow beings.
I wonder what halos of angels will be broken,
In the race to recover from the confusion,
To clear the way for a brighter conclusion.

War and peace an anvil of an age,
But the perception of the reader to mind the writer's way,
What pure bullshit is written in places such as these,
It does fill in time, a measure of confusion.

A many-coloured land is what this earth is,
The part of which is open and free so you see,
There is what is, what will, what can,
What maybe, probably most likely,
A sure thing to be a human alive to this.

ARC OF THE ANCIENTS

Am I writing a poem or a story?
I don't know but I do know this,
I am writing so that's it.

From the mouths of babes comes wisdom,
Or plenty of Vomit as some might call it,
But that's what we call a fine trick.
And that woman should clear that up,
Or the baby will surely drown in it.

So I have come to the end as the paper,
Is running short,
When it catches up I'll start again.

Written on? /8/86 (2.10 PM) Aged 22

THE REALITY OF A DREAM

As sleep descends bringing the curtain of reality down on our minds,
That shall open the curtains below,
The unconscious world of the dream to descend the steps,
You will find a story that can only be told in the light of reality,
So we call in logic that makes it a dream.

Open that door, the light brightens and you step,
Into a world of the mind and the power to create,
Your own kind of reality,
The world takes shape to a dream of conflict.

145

Two lights that glow in the shadows of a dark sky,
Above the world on a plane of light,
Blue and purple are the colours of one,
The other red and green,
Swords they hold in their hands,
Welding swiftly through the air,
In a acrobatic style,
That makes a rainbow of a sky.

They fought as consumed by a battle of mind,
The swords the instruments of their time,
With grace and beauty they fight,
But it is a struggle for their souls
That is at stake and the price is a life.

A night of struggle,
These powers evenly matched,
But a victor must be for the bond of reality,
Must be kept or the fighters will be,
Trapped in a circle that would never end.

Anger starts to assert and the light is tinged,
In a blackness that makes the plane shudder,
The light of blue and purple finds the edge,
And strikes the fatal blow as the anger,
Is blown away as the light of red and green
Fails in the frustration and fades into,
The reality from which it came to die.

The arm that welded the sword comes down,
The sword slipping from his grasp,
To vanish into the substance of his mind.

Battered and bruised the light a little distorted,
Shows the scars he now holds,
An eye of light pulsating red and now black,
He starts the journey back.

Through the door to ascend the steps,
In shock he returns even as sadness descends,
Why and who came to do battle,
In the mind of my dream?

146

ARC OF THE ANCIENTS

In my dream the answer still dwells,
From the battle first won,
And the other that still waits for my return,
The dream is the reality to come,
And the fight brought forth,
Now I wait to do battle or make peace.

Written on 3/11/86   Aged 22

MY BIRTHDAY

The day did start early with the tele,
I watched then was amused,
Then a discussion on rape and murder of children,
Great I thought trying to cheer me up?
But I watched and listened like a fool,
Feeling useless as the tears.

Then snap the switch goes and I speed up,
To arrive out of bed,
Dressed all prim and proper,
With pullover and trousers of blue,
To the shops I go – the paper,
I read of funnies and somber again,
Then the daft and silly things said under stars and things.

Walking to work to finish a job,
I happily skip my way there,
HA! HA! In work a surprise I receive,
Of gifts and cards asunder,
I glow with pleasure and a laugh to the lips,
Pleasure and full of beans I go back to the shops.

147

I aspire to the heights of three floors,
There are records of music and more shiny things,
Oh like Christmas joy with birthday joy,
All in the course of a day.
Then down stairs I gallop,
The bank is the horizon after,
Money laid to rest, and then back home I go.

Inside I listen to the music I have brought,
With money I can ill afford,
But I feel good so who gives a sod – I do not!

Then from there I go to Jackie's,
The tall limbed red haired lady of a few doors down,
A drink of wine and pleasant tidings,
Happy birthday to me – Great!

At 5.30 I leave to go home again,
Listen to some more music of pure joy,
Then busy to make ready to go to the outside world,
A taxi I take – in darkness but with lights to lead the way,
Arrive at Maria's home,
A hug and kiss greet me at the door,
And sausages that do fry and sizzle.

Her dinner I see, then a lamp that needs my attention,
A bulb I brought, in goes to the socket,
She forgets to turn off the electric,
Maybe she tries to fry me!

But remember she does and is quick on her feet,
So all is well and the light does shine.

Then a little later a walk to Steve's and Cathy's,
A drink of whiskey and messages to and fro,
More greetings and happiness to go my way,
Good init!

Then I run, far to go to the next place to see,
More friends,
Ah Ed and Linda, a bonus Ken,
A mountain of cards and gifts do I find,

ARC OF THE ANCIENTS

The heart that is behind it all is more than can be said.

The words from poems and messages bring overwhelming joy,
ME! They do bring me these words, these gifts!
ME of all people!
Are they sure? No mistake!!

No words except thankyou my fiends.
You gave me a birthday!

Written on 28/11/86   Aged 23

For My Friends

I WANDER

In a wilderness I travel,
Far and long in a desert of sand under my feet,
Oh magic of stars in lights do surround,
In glitter of mind and so falsely they hang.

My feet are heavy my mind does follow,
I look upon my sand in hills and valleys,
So quiet is the air filled by music and laughter,
To myself I find an oasis that's travels far and wide,
Drinking at the waterside.

Heavy is the heart, and drags me down,
To my feet I now crawl with blistering hands,
Sweat on the brow,
A hard job I do make of traveling down the road,
I could forsake.

A meaning I do need,
The mind does inquire,
For why is the passion in the sand,
That slips through my fingers and trickles down,
Like stardust, which it is, and not just sand that I see.

Open my eyes that are hopelessly closed,
For when I started a dream I did see,
A dream of new and glorious days of a world,
Remade in the new and better way.

But on this long journey road I slipped,
From my yellow brick road,
So the sand does welcome feet made of sand,
That is my choice to taste a different land.

The dunes do fade and sand fades away,
A look back yonder and flowers do bloom,
For we wander to and fro,
And slip and slide,
But when we can we learn to change our feet,
We can experience the new.

My yellow brick road does lie before me,
I do hesitate to continue on my dreams,
True journey.

Yes, I wait awhile on the edge of infinity,
And there I see a shadow,
Of myself in the clearing,
He does travel on my road, and he must,
Go forward, why wait, I must go to my land,
That does await my return.

One leap I make and I found my shadow,
And now one I do become,
He in its rightful place and I at mine.

Written on 13/12/86   Aged 23

MARIA

A long time ago in a far distant land,
I once saw a girl with big brown eyes,
That held the promise of things to come,
Of laughter and the tears that were bound to be.

Oh girl so small, but she walks so tall,
My heart journeyed to welcome but the strings,
Attached did start to pull and a parting we made,
To heal our pain and fathom the differences of our love.

You my crystal heart, a jewel in ice,
When emotion to give did freeze in the night,
By bats on the wing and the teeth that are bared,
And blood which is drawn to pay our price for the fare.

So the days did pass into weeks,
To the months that we did not share,
But a day was about to dawn when we met,
Again and found a friendship to belong.

Lessons in life we found on our way,
So in moments of time we could come together,
To share and heal our wounds together.

We are a combination to stir the stars in the heavens,
And turn suns into novas when we,
Dance naked in the clover!

Okay so we didn't its artistic hope,
Oh and how come you take your clothes off,
Everytime I come round,
Oh yes – sorry for your massage,
You like my healing hands,
So close but always just not far enough.

Written on 13/12/86   Aged 23

For Maria

ANGELINA

The spirit of the free is captured in the three,
The years she has graced our world,
The energy of the mighty is within,
Each clench of her tiny fists,
Fight I will – Challenge your heart,
She declares with every breath.

A stream – a trickle of emotion can she squeeze,
From any heart that is cold,
But for the most of us a fountain is born,
To shower upon her fair heart.

Her art is to push the keys that open souls,
No resistance can be met from her eyes of infinite charm,
Our eyes are now open and we see this little lady,
Of dynamite ready to blow our minds apart,
But always ready to put back together again,
With her versatile hands,
Which brings her glee of joy,
When we know that nothing is ever quite the same as before!

There is only one,
More would be too much,
Even asking is far to much,
No! You don't believe?!!
Then come and see,
For Angelina is her name,
An angel you may see,
But watch for the little devil inside her!!

Written on 14/12/86   (1.25pm) Aged 23

For Angelina

ONE WEEK TO CHRISTMAS

Its one-week to Christmas and here I am,
Sitting in the seat of red in front of a gas fire,
Some people are fast asleep,
But I'm quite awake talking to friends,
Of Christmas and all the fairies and stars,
And Santa to fill our dreams.

Cats that sit and watch,
Cleaning up after their day,
Music drifts through the air,
To tickle our ears of love and hope,
The best of all people,
My friends Linda and Ed.

Discussing their future,
To the baby in movement in the safest womb,
Liquid it swims ready to burst into the world,
And bring the light of another being,
And the idea of new life.

Chapters do close and open,
Beings dance in the heavens,
Wind blows the pages of thought,
Of books written in the tapestry of stars
And they speak of my friends,
Linda and Ed.
Go in dance to your bed!

Written on 18/12/86 Aged 23

For Linda and Ed

SHAKESPEARE AND SIR. EDMUND

The travelers of time as two people,
Oh Ed and myself to visit a peer,
Of his art of the written word,
But we do have gifts to bring our weary friend,

Yes You! Oh Shakespeare,
Parcels of words gift-wrapped and ready,
For you to absorb.

Daring are we, chuckle we do in,
Delight of faces in future to appear,
When they listen to you from your stage,
For we have a secret to stir the bones of dead men,
In their tatty clothes.

We step off the staircase of time,
In cottage of an ancient world,
There we see Shakespeare on his knees.

"Words oh words, where art thou,
Words on winter's night,
For thou has left me,
Oh I do despair!"

As two kings we bare all our gifts,
To shine on quill of pen,
So words again can march,
To war and slay all who go before you.

Arise Sir Edmund teach the master,
And so all shall know,
That thy Shakespeare can become the teacher,
Of all the little men,

A pen of modern age does come,
To hand and scribble and transform,
So the birth on a wing a bird,
Of words to tell a story,
Of those called Romeo and Juliet.

I took Sir Edmund to help thy master,

ARC OF THE ANCIENTS

Shakespeare with his books,
To tell of plays in,
The tragedy of loves sweet bitter sword.

The hour does approach for us to leave,
A now smiling Shakespeare off his knees,
Proclaiming for all to see,
"Your name Sir Edmund shall go down in history,
Go now and ply thy talent and make the paper,
Appear to breathe."

So at the end of this little late,
A message I now leave,
If you read a work,
Of majestic literacy,
Watch out as it breaks,
If nothing else you will pee
At the madness of Sir Edmunds Biography!

Written on 19/12/86 Aged 23

FOR EDMUND

ALONE AM I

Here I am, all alone, my heart cries,
In the pain of the needed love,
I am so sad my heart torn into pieces,
Of a heart broken by the tears of despair.

Please, oh please relieve my pain,
I need, yes I need! A girl, a woman,
To fulfill me.
Cry the tears that splash on the pages of all my thoughts,
The ink runs into a pattern that spells I am alone.

Warmth of a body – the woman I need,
To stop the pain of my empty space,
In my mind.

Do not pity me for I must be one of many,
Who sit and wish for love.

I have waited an age and nothing seems,
To bear any fruit, the seeds fall on stony ground.

Please I beg! I plead to my heart,
Help to salvage and bring to me my love.
I find nothing in the wells of water that say,
"Go search and you will find!"
I have haven't I!!
But all I hear is the reply to give me heartache,
I am alone, I am alone.

Is it lust? Is it just a body need?
And is it all I have feared?
To be just me and no woman to share my life,
To become one with hers.

A woman, a vision of satin in white,
Blond is her hair, blue eyes to slip into,
To splash to the depth to feel the cool water,
And the warmth it brings.

I see her but she sees every other,
A friend I am but no sun do I shine,
For her eyes.

So I search and fly to the sun for the experience,
That means a love I can trust,
Not to be taken away but to bear a fruit,
That proclaims we belong together.

I now leave my heart, I now must go,
To search the heavens for my love,
Then to earth to see the reality,
Of all my hope held in this aching heart.

156

ARC OF THE ANCIENTS

I return to the home of empty spaces,
Knowing that no arms are waiting,
To caress me,
My body cries only that familiar song,
All alone am I.

Tears that are spilt are the wasted hope,
Of dreams.
So now I come to you,
To slay the dragon of my dreams.

I need – I must find the one I can love,
To free my heart, to fly on the current,
Of air to feel the breeze on my cheek,
To know that I am not alone,
That I can shine,
For all that is to come,
To the triumph of my life.

So all I leave is hope,
That the day will dawn and bring a rainbow,
To a pot of gold that is the heart of the one,
I can love.
For that is my entire wish in the reflection,
Of my tear that says,
"I'm still alone!!!!!"

Written on 23/12/86   (11.55pm) Aged 23

THE HEALING

Healing the pain away from our bodies,
Our minds to bring the calm and peace of mind,
Injury does happen every day and so we fall in every way,
Body so hurt and torn apart a kind person came,
With a skill to stitch and bind you together again.

157

Fit and healthy there you now stand,
With your body well healed and ready to run,
Swift like the wind strong as a bull,
Your body is now one but you could be in for a fall.

I stand here also really healthy and pleased,
For I was there not an age ago,
A fine young person fit in my body,
But there was one thing I can now tell,
My mind was like a broken shell.

So fragile it was but I thought not,
And so I ran and played like all us fools,
Under a sun and upon sweet grass,
Until I fell and was shocked apart.

Now a strange thing happened my body did fail,
But my mind did mend and from the pain could be learnt,
To tell me a thing or ten.

Over these years did things begin,
And as my mind developed and found my ways,
And all the path did have their pain,
My mission came my mission went,
And my body did feel so spent.

I did think of one strange way I could explain,
For my mind to mend and build up again,
It drained my body to make me still,
And so the lessons did stay,
I filled with an appetite for learning,
Instead of shirking.

I once said if I could not find my way,
In the physical world I would become,
A pupil of my mind and soul,
To flex and stretch those other muscles.

To find the healing way and to turn my pain,
Into bright new days I found my mind,
And began to toy with myself,
An act of mental masturbation.

158

ARC OF THE ANCIENTS

I started this poem about you,
But found myself on the loo,
One good crap and with a splash,
Found my grip and raised myself,
To turn and gaze into my face.

I can heal with my hands to help,
The physical and mental minds,
Of those I live and bind my world,
Together with something new,
And so could you.

Written on 1/2/87   (11.45pm) Aged 23

REFLECTIONS
(*Never finished!*)

I a baby born in the land of life,
Sired from my parents who made it sworn,
Scream little child in the heat of the night,
Blazing stars shine,
The sky split in two with light in the heavens,
Scream of the night,
With storm wind blows in the breath of life.

Hope springs in the fountain of the womb,
Life signs and flesh is torn,
What of this baby trail of birth?
Then marked upon the forehead,
With the sigh of the damned.

Uncertain of goals I should reach,
Making the ladder for me to climb,
But is it the ghost of memories
Sworn in the mouths of parents to fade.

By coming into the sanity they preach,
Mixed by an insanity they seek,
Murder little child,
For I am hope sworn to change,
The world of my sires,
So it became the madness they eat,
And sorry little child for ill are the mother and father,
Sworn to beat my life I dare to reach.

Struggle struggling up the slope,
Nails on hands torn and bled,
Scraping the skin on the knees,
Mind dull and hiding from,
The hands that reach to pull me,
The child from my climb for life.

Day and day to month through month,
Into the years I make the grade to survive,
And speak the words to beat,
Away the hands I've sworn to survive,
Crying for my life.

My year is now four and birth is,
Celebrated on this day I have learnt,
I have seen – I know that they now
Have chains ready to bind me,
For they fear me now,
So I ran – run as a child,
Who learns that freedom is now my dream,
Flying in the darkness of each day,
And to feel the free air I now breathe.

Sight in the attic, I have the torture,
Of my dreams,
Colour haunts me in the shapes of horror,
 The dancing grin that is my life,
They may break me but that is only as real,
As the wishes of those that dream a,
Nightmare I now see,
The body may die but they can never have my soul,
For that is mine to keep.

ARC OF THE ANCIENTS

Happiness I wish for,
Love in the arms I seek,
To be held in honesty,
And lay the danger aside for a little peace,
As I drift through their world,
Never part but I blow each spark,
To light a fire of happiness,
I now strive to feel that part,
Is part of their whole life.

Moments stolen from them is my flame,
That warms the growing cold and hardness,
I have in my heart,
Survive I will,
For they now keep me in the cold embrace,
Of shame and misery of the failure,
Of my body.
Nightmare they keep me in,
But they may one day be learnt for me,
To break free.

My year is now eight, and they that speak,
Tear the heart out of my life and travel to an
Alien world that has a sea that now speaks,
In the roar of the waves of my personal,
Pain the height I may one day reach.
They still bind me but they lose a little more of me,
To the dreams I keep.

On sandy beach and slot machine days,
I now walk to find my way,
To forget the shame and search the sky,
For signs to say,
"Its over now, you have no more to fear,
Have your little peace."
Futile dream – quicksand sleep,
I find no peace.

Danger lurks on prowling streets,
On moonlit nights and warm dreamy blue-sky days,
I find another way.
From boys who search through a broken door,

Stolen toys – hidden store,
Policeman walks,
Betrayer in our little world,
Split the sweet sand in the hand of man.

Adventure starts in a run, run from fear,
A band of souls in tattered shoes see,
The fields and like mice we run,
On darkest night with,
Mud caked shoes, weary hearts,
We turn back and face the wrath,
Of those that mean to hurt us.

Hero night I from indifferent eyes,
To angry father,
The victim I am so I slaughter,
To milk this moment I now save,
For all time of my days,
Is this the only way to make it felt?
That I have a place,
In family life,
And I am worth some emotion that says,
They care.
I hugged the thought in my bed for many days,
Until a time came and I tried it again.

Caught in violent pain and nothing more,
Just the soak filled pillow of my tears,
An aching heart and I swore,
That if I chanced to run away,
I would do all never to be caught again.

My year is now eleven.......

Written on 9/3/87 Aged 23

Authors Note: In The Great Storm 1987 my life changed, and it took me on a
path that the following year would change my life for ever!

162

ALPHA to OMEGA to ALPHA

STARING INTO THE EYES OF ETERNITY

In the last few months I have sat on the edge of a cliff, staring deep into the unknown depths. Sometimes I have fallen up, falling down becomes up and the empty space is filled with anticipation, as the rules once perceived now like a waterfall cascading over and into. Making the spaces in-between my vibrations ripple outwards wrapping me in colour that touches me as I fall. Thoughts are simple and direct but complex in a humorous spin that makes me laugh even as my body feels the nausea as I let go. Knowing why angels don't need wings.

Almost a year has past since I learnt that this cliff was to be home, as I used my will to change the rules even as my body cried No! Shedding weight to make me lighter sounds reasonable if I am to land in Eternity safe and whole. Is that what my body tells my mind as it sheds itself of the unwanted. I feel lighter; almost three stones have been consumed to keep me alive or just part of the process? Almost seven days without food, no desire to try, when forced to by me to override to make the desire for food true once more and the body sheds it as soon as it hits the lake in the darkness of my stomach. That is such a small place now even as the cliff becomes more shadow the reality of the edge breaking down. Five weeks since my body began to reject even the slightest morsel. Tried to make it not so.

The pain of failing muscle, bones, of heart, lungs, kidneys and now the liver, were the reasons for pills to be taken, then Eleven days ago it seemed to ease, and I had four days without pills, the pain managed once more like the days and months before. So I rolled away from the cliff top and stood, trembling that once more I can move away and leave the eyes of Eternity for another time and place. Then like a hammer blow my right side, once immune to the worst of the pain now vulnerable imploded and something deep inside my brain broke. On my knees, whimpering like a sad puppy, as the pain broke apart my defences and with tears trying to stop the madness of cries I rocked like a baby clutching a cushion for comfort and desperate hands kneading it to distract my mind from breaking. Half my face frozen, speech more a dribble like the drool betraying me, as the eyes of Eternity grow large with anticipation bidding me to let go.

Doctor! Doctor! Doctor! But not I, as being poked and prodded was not my desire, just the pills to be taken again and hope that this pain isn't overwhelming. They helped and sitting on the edge of the cliff once more, the throbbing in my head the pain in my eyes was managed. Sometimes the wind howls and rocks me but still

I sit to see if I can move away once more. Today three lots of pills allow me to sit and type, my stomach rolls like I was on a ship but I keep the focus even as the eyes of Eternity can be felt. They call strong tonight but I do not look.

When I close my eyes at night Eternity is stronger and they gaze at me watching me, waiting to see if I will open my eyes in the morning. We both wait, both as calm now with each other like slippers well worn and comfortable. All the things that were done last year in the just in case moments are done, the contacting of family and friends this year is done. All is known but unknown, those that care, do and those that don't stay away. Joined with those that care but are too frightened to want to see or to think or to feel the hopelessness that comes from knowing there is nothing they can do to fix it. In the end all those that know the seat on the edge of Eternity know all they want is a hand to hold so that they know they don't have to be brave alone.

I no longer have questions of courage inside me, or doubt of how will I cope? Just the doing, the making, the sharing of moments that make me wink into the eyes of Eternity, for if I am to embrace you then I will do so willingly when my will can no longer embrace my body. Someday there will be a time when staring into the eyes of Eternity will only be the moment before I embrace you, then you will know, and I will know why you stare with such hope into mine own. But that day has not yet come, and my fingers typing this show that I am still here sitting on the edge, sometimes falling up but always landing down to feel the earth beneath my feet once more while you keep staring into the eyes of Eternity.

Written while this book was being prepared for publication. Tuesday, 04 March 2003 Martin A Enticknap

ARC OF THE ANCIENTS

About The Author:

Martin A Enticknap, poet, and author of *Exodus - The Dolph/in Saga* He is also a computer graphic artist ,his creations include the wrap round covers of *Exodus – The Dolph/in Saga and the Arc of The Ancients.*

(Also Covers of *Heritage Findings Of Atlantis* and *Overcoming Asperger's – Personal Experience & Insight* by Robert S Sanders Jnr).

He lives on the peaceful island of Sanday, Orkney. He cares deeply for the environment and has a special empathy for Cetaceans. In the past he has swum in all weathers, around the year and has swum many times with seals, from one of the common seal colonies that share the island. He says, " Even in the coldest sea you *really* can feel the warmth of those that dwell within its relaxing embrace or was that just the effect of hypothermia?!!"

The Author's first novel Exodus – The Dolph/in Saga is a highly original fantasy novel which really captures the imagination. A book to read if you would like to be enchanted by something magically different. Feel its gentle harmonies and let yourself flow with this book and you will find yourself transported to a whole new world. You will never look at Dolphins and Whales in quite the same way again. If your curiousity has been Aroused and you want to dip into the world of Mel-e-gar and Tan-e-lea then you can obtain a copy from www.amazon.com or www.amazon.co.uk

Reviews from the Important People - The Readers!

From: Zoz 10/12/2001
on **THE CRUCIBLE OF CHANGES**

I love this, especially from verse three to the second last one. Powerful stuff.

From: Jenny 3/19/2001
on **FOOTSTEPS OF GAIA**

As usual you've picked a very interesting and mysterious subject which leaves me itching to know more. You have a gift for story telling and for teasing the imagination.

From Bladerunner 17/01/2001
on **KYRIE ELEISON**

A haunting poem, although some of it is very mysterious.

From Jenny (Wales)17/01/2001
on **KYRIE ELEISON**

Very chilling . . . This poem is clever because it doesn't appear to be that 'dark' at first glance, but having read it, I found my fingertips had gone cold.

From Shona 12/16/2001
on **RIDING THE PALE HORSE**

Plenty of images. I love the line about the flag of stars drifting on the breath of a goddess.

From Cat 06/01/2001
on **WINTER'S WATER-TIME**

Your poem is amazingly beautiful, and so sad. I absolutely loved it.

From Suzzie : 05/07/2002
on **"When They Ask"**

As the author of such a moving and eloquent poem, I enjoyed the way you play with metre and rhyme...it takes a very accomplished poet to do that.

From Julie : 7/1/2001
on **I HAD A DREAM**

I thought it was very romantic even though their hands got cut off!!!

From Autumn 08/01/2001
on **JUST MAD**

loved this! I've enjoyed reading your work. And isn't being a child disguised as an adult great fun!!!???

From Mez 10/01/2001
on **NO CUDDLY LOVELY BEAR**

This is very very sad and harrowing, and it makes one sad and angry at the same time.

From the Pleasure Dome a home for writers on MSN

www.ingramcontent.com/pod-product-compliance
Lightning Source LLC
Chambersburg PA
CBHW031844090426
42741CB00005B/347